The Glorious Fourth of July

The Glorious Fourth of July

OLD-FASHIONED TREATS AND TREASURES FROM AMERICA'S PATRIOTIC PAST

Diane C. Arkins

PELICAN PUBLISHING COMPANY
GRETNA 2009

The word "Pelican" and the depiction of a pelican are trademarks of Pelican Publishing Company, Inc., and are registered in the U.S. Patent and Trademark Office.

Library of Congress Cataloging-in-Publication Data

Arkins, Diane C.
  The glorious Fourth of July : old-fashioned treats and treasures from America's patriotic past / Diane C. Arkins.
      p. cm.
  Includes bibliographical references.
  ISBN 978-1-58980-611-5 (hardcover : alk. paper) 1. Fourth of July. 2. Fourth of July celebrations. I. Title.
  E286.A1252 2009
  394.2634—dc22
                                2008048812

Spine: Vintage 4" Uncle Sam decorative die-cut ca. 1918 by Dennison Manufacturing Co.

Printed in Singapore
Published by Pelican Publishing Company, Inc.
1000 Burmaster Street, Gretna, Louisiana 70053

With deepest affection for all of canine kind: may loving homes be found for one and all.

Vintage postcard "Miss Liberty" at night marked "The Photo-Color-Graph Co. New York No. 200/4." Mailed Dunelle, New Jersey, July 1, 1909.

CONTENTS

For Starters
Preface 9

The New and More Glorious Fourth of July
A Brief History of "The Day We Celebrate" 15
Community Celebrations: A Good
Time for One and All 24
I Love a Parade . . . A Photo Album 37
Fireworks Fever 40

Parties in the "Old-Fashioned" Way
How Inviting! 52
Three Cheers for the Red, White, and Blue Décor 55
Do Me a Favor: Party Novelties with Panache 65
Food for the Fourth 73
Dressing the Patriotic Part 90
Memories of the "New and More Glorious"
Fourth . . . A Photo Album 96
Let Us Entertain You: Party Games and Other Amusements 99

Grand Finale
Feting the Fourth in Rhyme and Season 105
It Was a Grand Old Day 115
Resource Guide 116

Vintage embossed postcard maked "Copyright 1908 P. Sander,
N. Y." Mailed Peoria, Illinois, July 2 (year illegble).

PREFACE

"Hurrah for the Fourth of July! Wave the banners, beat the drums, bring on the speech-making, shows, contests, games and parades. Let us on this occasion recall the brightness of its honors and seek to impress upon ourselves and others our faith in its principles and achievements. The privileges for which men died and women sacrificed, the acquisitions of long years of struggle for the right, although become so familiar that we seldom recognize this beneficence, deserve no slight commemoration. Show forth the sincerity of your citizenship, unselfishly, unrestrainedly . . . with the exhilaration of conviction, that the memory of our hallowed foundation 'may not perish from the land.'"

The Household Magazine, July 1914

Ahhh . . . the Glorious Fourth of July—that familiar day of patriotic spirit, backyard barbecues, and Uncle Sam.

Hooray! for the parades and the marching bands.

Huzzah! for the glittery tinsel of fireworks against inky black skies.

Don't forget to salute the flag and while you're at it, pour yourself a refreshing glass of ice-cold lemonade.

Yes, *our* Glorious Fourth of July. With a salute, a BANG! and an ample infusion of all things red, white, and blue, Americans have (with somber exceptions during times of war and/or national emergency) always reveled in celebrating the nation's birthday with high style. Yet, even as people employ thoroughly *high-tech* methods to help them draw up their July 4 plans today, they appear to be smitten with the idea of celebrating the day in a decidedly *old-fashioned* way. A quick Internet-based search (done when the holiday is close at hand) is likely to yield *millions* of options for "old-fashioned Fourth of July," all delivered in a seemingly impossible fraction of a second!

The founding fathers would no doubt be impressed.

And so it seems clear that patriotic Americans from Savannah to Seattle are captivated by the perceived charms of Independence Days gone by. Nostalgic notions aside, though, *exactly what is an "old-fashioned Fourth?"*

Welcome to *The Glorious Fourth of July: Old-Fashioned Treats and Treasures from America's Patriotic Past*, a virtual scrapbook of mementoes and memories of the merry ways the nation's birthday was celebrated in the late 1800s and early 1900s. Filled with evocative images of patriotic memorabilia, period photographs, and colorful examples of the artistically illustrated postcards of the era, the book presents a collection of July 4 entertainments as they originally appeared—flowery turns of phrase, meandering prose, antiquated spelling and all—in turn-of-the-twentieth-century books, newspapers, and popular women's magazines.

Interestingly, the Fourth of July itself has traditionally been a holiday in flux. As much as the day brings us together to define and unite us as a people, Independence Day has always been (and is likely to remain) an ever-evolving occasion with a history of dissent. Over the decades, "The Day We Celebrate" has served as a "magnet" of sorts for those seeking to organize and bring attention to matters of significant national importance: partisan strife, regional conflicts, civil rights, the evils of alcohol, labor issues, women's concerns, class struggles, and child welfare amongst them. These diverse and admittedly complex aspects of our Fourth of July have been ably recounted in myriad fascinating books of recent vintage.

That said, America in the early twentieth century was also a time when you made your own fun in ebullient fashion, and when things were homemade more often than not. It was an age of genteel manners, grand formality, and visible patriotism. It was also an era marked by Fourth of July celebrations that boasted some unexpected menu choices (making those genteel manners all the more important when faced with second helpings of questionable party food) and, most notably, ushered in an end to some of the most ill-considered and dangerous ways of all time with regard to the use of fireworks. (On this latter score, **it should be noted** that this book presents genuine glimpses

Vintage embossed postcard marked "PFB No. 8252." Mailed East Pittsburgh, Pennsylvania, June 16, 1908.

of American cultural history *as they were recorded in their time* and, further, that the mere act of recounting history does not imply in any way that it should be emulated. With particular regard to fireworks and related materials, *it is the individual and the individual alone who, with all due regard for modern safety considerations and the tenets of common sense, bears complete responsibility for his/her own actions and resultant consequences.*)

The vintage materials presented herein will acquaint readers with a history of the Fourth of July that deserves to be not simply *savored,* but *saved* as well. The amazing modern technology (online auctions and improved access to library holdings amongst them) that makes it easier than ever before to connect with older published material also, regrettably, seems to contribute to its demise: to wit, as today's libraries increase their dependency on computerized forms of information, they significantly reduce their holdings in traditional "hard" formats. Many institutions now fail to retain physical copies of magazines beyond a single year! . . . and some choose to relinquish aging but still useful microfilm and ancillary equipment as well.

Speaking as someone who used to revisit library copies of Beatles-era issues of *Seventeen* long after having reached that fabled age herself, and who now enthuses over genuine ca. 1895 copies of *The Queen of Fashion* and others like them, I find this trend toward virtual *everything* to be disconcerting. Nothing compares to actually holding a book or magazine of any vintage as it's being read.

The tendency to dismiss that which is "old" is in itself not new. *"It has always been a source of regret to me to see the careless way in which people treat their old magazines,"* wrote a fellow magazine aficionado, in the April 1911 issue of *The Designer Magazine.* But modern inclinations to eliminate so much physical reference material "because we have it online" should serve as a warning to those designated keepers of the past: thoughtful consideration should always be directed to preservation plans before little

Spirited canine reveler. Vintage early twentieth-century photograph.

Vintage embossed postcard. Postally unused.

or nothing of the past remains to even consider discarding.

So read on . . . and while you're at it, have yourself a merry little (bonus) Independence Day celebration now. After all, those ever-glorious Fourths of yesteryear were entertaining enough to merit second helpings of all the old-fashioned fun they entailed.

How to Enjoy Yourself on the Day of Patriotism and Noise

Excerpted from *The New York Times*, July 4, 1893

"*I don't know what to do this Fourth,*" said the young man with the brown hat and eyeglasses to his neighbor in the elevated train. The neighbor was an older man who stopped reading his newspaper, pulled off his spectacles, and said, reflectively:

Don't have more fun than you can handle.

Don't consider the hot weather a personal affront to yourself. Other persons are perspiring also.

Don't try to show everybody else how he ought to set off his firecrackers.

Don't expect your boy to fire his crackers in the nice tin pan you have arranged for him. He is doing the business, and he knows what gives him the most fun.

Don't play a firecracker joke on your wife or any other girl in a muslin frock. Women are such strange creatures that they might object.

Don't put on too many airs about being bored by your holiday. They will know you are dissembling.

Don't plan to have a nice, quiet day of it all. You will only be disappointed.

Don't swear at the punk.

Don't apply hot and rebellious liquors to your blood.

Don't eat too much lobster with your ice cream and lemon pie.

Don't make bathing suit jokes.

Don't hurry. You can do that any day.

Don't tell long stories about the fine lot of fireworks you had last year.

Don't abuse a policeman for obeying his orders.

Don't select the president of a fire insurance company as a cheerful holiday companion on July 4.

Don't expect your wife to enjoy herself exactly in the same way that you do. She also has an individual soul, and oftener than you think, knows just what she wants without instruction from you.

Vintage embossed postcard marked "Copyright 1908 P. Sander N.Y." Mailed Milwaukee, Wisconsin, July 5, 1909.

Don't expect to have as much fun as you used to have.

Don't behave with less general common sense than your own small boy.

The young man leaned back and grinned. "*All right,*" he said. "*I won't forget.*"

Vintage embossed postcard with shiny "gelatin" finish marked "0684." Mailed Lewiston, Maine, July 4, 1913.

A BRIEF HISTORY OF "THE DAY WE CELEBRATE"

"Everything was conducted with the greatest order and decorum, and the face of joy and gladness was universal. Thus may the Fourth of July, that glorious and ever memorable day, be celebrated throughout America by the Sons of Freedom from age to age till time shall be no more. Amen and amen."

The Pennsylvania Gazette, July 9, 1777

Ah, the Fourth of July, a day that was bestowed with the noble mantle of "glorious" from that first anniversary celebration held in Philadelphia in 1777.

Glorious indeed. Observances of what would become popularly referred to as "The Day We Celebrate" were destined for greatness in spectacle and meaning from the very start. In a July 1776 letter to his wife Abigail, no less a patriotic luminary than John Adams described his thoughts on how the nation's birthday should be celebrated:

> I am apt to believe that it will be celebrated, by succeeding generations, as the great anniversary festival. It ought be commemorated, as the Day of Deliverance by solemn acts of devotion to God Almighty. It ought be solemnized with pomp and parade, with shews [shows], games, sports, guns, bells, bonfires and illuminations from one end of this continent to the other from this time forward forever more.

In actuality, Adams had directed these sentiments toward anniversary celebrations that he expected would be held on *July 2*, the date in 1776 when the Second Continental Congress "declared the United Colonies Free and Independent States." It wasn't until two days later, on the *fourth*, that Congress approved a final version of the Declaration of Independence and ordered it printed for distribution to the states: the date it bore was July 4, 1776.

(No one actually signed the document until August and the last remaining signatures weren't affixed until November).

But Adams's desires for pageantry, thanksgiving, and conviviality to hallmark annual observances of America's independence were borne out by first-year festivities that included prayers, public rejoicing and bell ringing, speeches and toasts, communal banquets and formal private dinners, music and concerts, military displays and musket fire, bonfires and "illuminations" (the popular practice of setting windows aglow with candles), and, of course, fireworks.

Such *let-the-eagle-scream* bravado set the tone for Fourth of July celebrations held during the Republic's early years, a time when the observances were meant to recapture the spirit of the revolution—after all, the nation remained at war with England until 1783—and help foster a cohesive national identity. Calls for unity faltered when, beginning in the late 1780s, separate Independence Day observances were staged by groups with differing political agendas; divisiveness continued to mar the day until the nation was again politically united following the further armed conflict with Britain during the War of 1812.

Throughout the nineteenth century, America's birthday continued to be feted with customs that blended solemn reflection and thanksgiving with showier activities like military parades, artillery salutes, music, picnics, and formal feasting. Traditions like these, along with other more novel diversions such as circuses, balloon ascensions, horseracing, and fishing expeditions, represented the "old-fashioned Fourth of July" ideal that Americans sought to emulate as early as the waning years of the nineteenth century.

Public displays of fireworks, of course, were still an integral part of the Fourth, but by this time, the established cacophony of gunpowder and sulfur had been joined by more raucous accomplices that afforded users the dual temptations of delicious danger and oh-so-satisfying noise. Such were the charms of completely unregulated *private* fireworks.

Though joyous noise had indeed been part of John Adams's original celebratory mandate, the brouhaha generated by "backyard patriots" grew ever more

Vintage embossed postcard. Postally unused.

bothersome—and dangerous—with each passing decade. From dawn on July 4 (if not late at night on the third), the rowdies and the mischievous, primarily thrill-seeking young men and small boys, filled the day with the *BANG!*, *fizzzz*, *P-O-P*, whistle, *C-R-A-S-H*, and *whir-r-r-r* of firecrackers, pinwheels, sky rockets, and the like. The resultant mayhem tormented legions of fearful, sleep-deprived citizens.

"We all dread the coming of the Fourth of July now," wrote author and social commentator George William Curtis in *Harper's New Monthly Magazine* (1854). He further stated:

> There was a time when the very name was melodious with sweet promise [but] that enthusiasm is long since flown away in villainous saltpetre, exploded in firecrackers, and whizzed to the empyrean in skyrockets. They are weary and noisy days now. . . . We hope [they] will end without Freddy's being blown up by his rockets and firecrackers. We stay within doors to escape the roar and the row; or we slip away to some kind friend in the country who will promise to protect us from ginger-pop and pistols.

Writing that same year, *The New York Times* concurred.

> A succession of sharp concussions, the smell of powder borne in upon the night air, an occasional sky rocket throwing its shower of sparks against the sky, and an incessant explosion of firecrackers—those stifling, deafening nuisances—gave warning that the "Glorious Fourth," The Anniversary of America's Independence, is about to burst upon us, with all its concomitants of noise, smoke, heat, music, rum and patriotism.

In order to escape the incessant commotion that—in the vernacular—"made the night hideous," citizens who could afford to do so began to abandon the cities in favor of feting the Fourth with more sedate country picnics or excursions bound for, as *The New York Times* would later brilliantly contend, "points where it was believed, or hoped, that the small boy existed only in small quantities or not at all." It was in no small way ironic that city dwellers were compelled to abandon their established routines to *gain liberty* from the very devices being used to *celebrate liberty* in the first place!

Vintage postcard marked "The Valentine & Sons' Publishing Co. Ltd." Postmarked twice, at Utica, New York, June 30, 1908, and Hartford, Connecticut, July 1, 1908.

Vintage embossed postcard marked "P. Sander."
Postally unused.

Victorian advertising trade card ca. 1890.

In 1859, *The Times* mused that "it is certainly rather a curious thing that...we should have hit upon no better way of celebrating the birth-day of our nation than by a clumsy imitation of the old Roman saturnalia" (a bacchanalian festival marked by riotous chaos) as the public at large became increasingly concerned about the devastation visited upon people and property from indiscriminate fireworks use. Newspapers published lengthy lists of shocking accidents and costly fires: a boy of five had his hand shattered by the explosive force of a miniature cannon; an eleven-year-old boy was shot through the hand by a pistol; a man was shot in the face and "one eye nearly put out;" a young girl was burned to death after her clothes caught fire from fireworks carelessly ignited by others.

By 1875, *The Chicago Tribune* bemoaned the "dark and dangerous" side of the holiday, observing, "ninety-nine successive years have we set aside one whole day for killing small boys, putting out eyes, rending limbs [and] scaring horses . . . as a glorification and symbol of the American idea of freedom." Some two decades later, frustrations, which were doubtless common to the majority, were expressed by one beleaguered individual who identified himself as "A Survivor" in his letter to the editor of *The New York Times*. "As we recede further and further from the original day and the spirit of the 'Glorious Fourth,' the noise of our celebrations becomes greater and more exasperating, and the number of casualties the larger in proportion to the increase [size-wise] of the patriot."

As lists of holiday-related tragedies grew, so did the size and power of personal fireworks and, with them, the overall danger they posed to users and innocent bystanders alike. There were heavy-duty 17.5-inch "toy" saluting cannons that propelled firecrackers (and were frequently overstuffed with inappropriate materials) and flimsy blank-shooting "toy" pistols that dramatically increased chances for seemingly inconsequential minor injuries that lead to deadly "patriotic"— or "Fourth of July"—tetanus (so called to differentiate it from the small number of tetanus cases attributable to other causes throughout the year). Tiny Chinese-made "ladyfinger" firecrackers were dwarfed by "bombs" and "rippers" possessed of "the power almost to raise the dead."

Larger still were four- to six-pound skyrockets "of the

variety previously seen only at professional fireworks exhibits . . . no one [had] thought of placing them on the general market [before now] as it was thought that average citizens would find them too expensive or too dangerous to shoot off at their front gates," and immensely powerful cannon crackers. The latter, manufactured in lengths up to fourteen inches and, amazingly, still intended for use by children, "sound pretty much like the blowing up of a powder magazine . . . [and] have been known to bring a policeman to the scene at top speed" (*The New York Times*, June 28, 1891).

Larger still grew the lists of accidents, fires, and deaths.

"The Fourth of July stands forth on the calendar conspicuous as the day on which little children are allowed to play with dynamite and gunpowder," fretted *The Ladies' Home Journal* . . . and justifiably so.

By the 1870s, cries for fireworks regulation began to be heard, but they were usually met by the laissez-faire "boys will be boys" shrugs of indulgent parents and/or adults who fondly recalled the firecracker-fueled antics in their own pasts. To top it off, the powerful and highly successful American fireworks industry—comprised of manufacturers that, in the late 1800s, made virtually all explosive novelties used in the entire country save the tiny "ladyfinger" crackers that were imported from China—perpetuated myths that their products posed no real hazards.

"Speaking of danger," crowed one bold merchant, "there is very little in any kind of fireworks . . . firecrackers are only made to frighten women and children."

To make matters worse, restrictions that *were* enacted usually couldn't be effectively enforced. The *New York Times* reported that the Fourth of July of 1891 was a time when "the irrepressible small boy, with no fear of the police before his eyes, was in his glory, and exploded firecrackers of all sizes and degrees of detonation in reckless fashion."

By the late nineteenth century, many fireworks had indeed become too big to handle without disastrous consequences and previously unheeded calls for reform began to reach sympathetic ears across the social spectrum.

"The American people are beginning to take a common-sense view of their duty in celebrating the [Fourth]," *The*

Vintage postcard. Mailed New Durham, New Jersey, July 4 (year illegible).

Pair of early-twentieth-century Fourth of July stereoview cards. Upper: "Celebrating the Great and Glorious 4th of July" marked no. 26(a); lower: "The Day After the 4th of July Celebration" marked no. 26(b).

Vintage postcard with embossed edges marked "Fourth of July Series No. 9." Postally unused.

Vintage postcard with embossed edges marked "Fourth of July Series No. 9." Postally unused.

Times reported in 1894. "Now that the country has fairly started on its second century there has apparently sprung up a feeling that patriotism does not call for so much burning of powder."

Initial steps on the road to what would eventually be christened the "New and More Glorious Fourth" were taken when, in 1899, *The Chicago Tribune* began to publish statistics of Independence Day injuries shortly after each year's toll was known in early July. By 1903, the American Medical Association began to compile more thoroughly vetted numbers each autumn and proceeded to report the grim results with mass mailings to newspapers and other publications across the nation.

 American women were also among the earliest supporters of fireworks reform—"*The protest against the general use of dangerous fireworks began with mothers and women with mother-hearts,*" observed *The Mother's Magazine* in 1910—and other influential reform-minded forces such as *The Ladies' Home Journal* and the Society for the Suppression of Unnecessary Noise chimed in. Finally in 1909, a concerted campaign to establish what was christened "A Safe and Sane Fourth of July" was instituted by the Playground Association of America, a group that sought to create more suitable environments in which youngsters could play.

Funded in part by a charitable foundation established by wealthy benefactor Mrs. Russell Sage, leaders of the Safe and Sane movement lobbied notable individuals in both the civic and private sectors to speak out with their endorsements of the concept. The campaign itself became a mix of carefully choreographed publicity, including colorful educational pamphlets and a well-received film short that depicted the sorrows caused by reckless fireworks use, and effective one-on-one action. Whenever possible, movement representatives made personal visits to assist individual communities in developing the programs they needed to replace the deeply ingrained "national bad habit" of July 4 fireworks.

"To keep the children from sighing for firecrackers or other more dangerous fireworks will be difficult to accomplish," *The New Idea Woman's Magazine* pointed out in 1909, "unless you offer them something as seductively entertaining [instead]." Consequently, agendas for Safe and Sane celebrations put a spotlight on child-friendly activities like youth parades, mass demonstrations of physical training and athletic competitions, carnivals, pageants and historical tableaux, flag drills, and essay contests. Fireworks remained a part of the celebrations but only in the form of professionally staged civic displays.

"New Fourth" agendas were also significantly influenced by citizens associated with the Progressive Movement, unaffiliated groups of individuals who sought to remedy the social problems brought on by industrialization and urbanization. When it came to the Fourth of July, progressives hoped to bring about a greater respect for democracy and American ways by instilling increased patriotism in native-born Americans while simultaneously motivating immigrants to abandon the over-the-top rowdiness (fireworks use and excessive drinking were targeted) they often displayed on the nation's birthday. Unsurprisingly, the road to safer, saner celebrations led once again to the active involvement of children.

"Youngsters whose names told of ancestors from Russia, Sweden, Norway or Poland touched elbows with those from families rooted in America since the Declaration was signed—and they were all vociferously and joyously America," attested a 1908 account of Fourth of July celebrations in Minneapolis. By the late 1910s, legions of children had participated in diversity-oriented Independence Day activities like folk dancing and parade of nation assemblies.

Other related efforts, such as reading the Declaration of Independence aloud in foreign languages and larger-scale parades of nations that also included adult participants, undertaken by those in the Progressive Movement manifested themselves in unrealized efforts to transform July 4, 1915, into "Americanization Day." This new day would be an occasion for citizenship receptions

Patriotic woman embraces the flag. Vintage photograph ca. 1920.

Vintage embossed postcard marked "International Art Publ. Co. Series No. 2443." Postally unused.

Vintage embossed postcard marked "Fourth of July Series No. 4." Postally unused.

and other activities devoted to showing "a gladness that we are Americans." Later, in the 1920s, the movement established a formal national "Citizenship Day" meant to uplift and inspire *all* Americans regardless of where they were born.

The concept of the "New Fourth" was evocatively summed up by *McCall's Magazine* in 1913:

> It is plain enough, then, what the new Fourth must be—the true, constructive, sane Fourth; the Fourth which we are to put in the place of the one which we have taken away. It must be a day in which we should give expression to what towns are doing toward making the national life such as the Signers of the Declaration of Independence dreamed that it would be. It must be a day of exercises, celebration, pageants which shall give form to what we have done, and what we long to do, make plain to our children the existence of a high civic ideal, the respect in which it is held by their elders, and their own part in maintaining its integrity.

Despite obstacles to antifireworks laws posed by the raucous old-world ways of some immigrants; native-born citizens who waxed nostalgia for the dangerous "old ways" of celebrating; and the powerful fireworks industry, which ultimately did see some makers go out of business, among them New York's Pain Fireworks Manufacturing Company, most adults were convinced that the time for change had indeed arrived. More and more cities hopped on the Safe and Sane bandwagon every year, and the results were dramatic as evidenced by the following report filed by *The New York Times* in 1910.

> Not in many a year had Brooklyn spent so noiseless a Fourth of July. The people of the borough—that is, the adult folk—took to the "safe and sane" notion like the proverbial duck to water. Entering into the new spirit of things, parents everywhere . . . withheld the conventional giant cracker, the torpedo, and other lockjaw producing explosives from little Jimmy and Mabel and listened not to their pleadings.
>
> The result was the ambulance surgeons and hospital nurses put in a dull day, the sick and tired and nervous folk enjoyed a rest, and the youngsters themselves came to know more about the real significance of the day—that it was something more than a mere excuse to make noise.

Comparative statistics compiled throughout the second decade of the twentieth century showed that the cumulative efforts of safe and sane programs led to a reduction of up to ninety-five percent in fireworks-related injuries and death. With their primary mission accomplished, most Safe and Sane Association chapters disbanded by 1920. Other groups, like the Safety First Federation of America and the National Fire Protection Association, continued to direct efforts toward improving Independence Day safety. The dedication of these and doubtless others that followed throughout the twentieth century led to the far more sensible laws and practices that govern our Independence Day celebrations today.

As times change, one man's "New Fourth" ultimately becomes another's vision of an old-fashioned holiday. Customs established in the bygone days of the early twentieth century built the framework for how we enjoy the holiday today. The history was colorful. The ideas were inspired. *This* was your great-grandfather's Fourth of July—get ready to *celebrate!*

Vintage embossed postcard marked "4021." Postally unused with recipient's name written in pencil on reverse.

COMMUNITY CELEBRATIONS

A Good Time for One and All

"What is your neighborhood going to do for the Fourth of July? Are half of you going to close your houses and depart for the seashore or country, leaving the other half at home to console themselves by burning up almost as much money in dangerous fireworks? Or are you considering, as so many communities are, a neighborhood celebration to include old and young, rich and poor?"

McCall's Magazine, July 1920

When reformers of the early 1900s promoted a "New and More Glorious Fourth of July," they realized that it was not enough to simply lobby for the elimination of dangerous fireworks. They recognized that for change to be successful, they also needed to promote more wholesome ways to celebrate the day. Lending an early, outspoken voice to efforts being made to publicize the dreadful human toll associated with unsafe fireworks, especially when it came to children, *The Ladies' Home Journal* offered the following ideas for updating agendas in 1907:

> One thing is certain: If the boys are expected to give up their fireworks it is only fair that they should have something very good instead. They like athletic contests, so arrange ball games, ball-throwing competitions, foot and bicycle races, cricket and tennis matches, archery contests . . . and offer prizes in all cases. Send up toy balloons, each having a card attached bearing a promise of good rewards for the first cards returned, and many children will ask for no better than to chase and search for balloons for hours.
>
> Girls may find certain mild excitement in striving for prizes for the best exhibits of red, white and blue flowers. Lawn parties, too, will please them, especially if they may attend in costume.

Enter the community-sponsored celebration, a place where down-home spirit and increased national pride inspired citizens to pull out all the stops to fete America's birthday with heart and style.

In big cities, reformers and organizers worked to develop Safe and Sane agendas that would ensure a good time for everyone while simultaneously embracing the founding fathers' visions of dignity and meaning. In 1916, the Mayor's Independence Day Committee in New York City allocated $25,000 (close to half a million dollars by 2008 standards) to its Safe and Sane Program. Its citywide agenda for youngsters included children's parades, patriotic exercises in the schools, and, under the auspices of the Department of Education and Public School Athletic League, mass demonstrations of physical and military training, athletics, and folk dancing.

Plans also called for nighttime illumination of public buildings, which was budgeted at $7,000, approximately $133,000 in 2008. Legions of red, white, and blue lanterns were suspended throughout in the neighborhoods. There were "Parisian night fetes" with large bands and street dancing, block parties, and professionally staged fireworks displays. Contributions from private citizens were encouraged to help with the costs.

But, if the Independence Day festivities that were staged in big cities represented the nation's patriotic heart, the celebrations that took place across small-town America spoke for its soul. In smaller communities, planning committees labored to add inventive touches to familiar customs as they offered residents fresh new amusements. Since picnics and parades were already cherished Independence Day traditions argued party planners across the board, why not make the day even merrier by encouraging celebrants to sport red, white, and blue attire, or to appear in novel costumes?

Sporting competitions, both regulation (fifty-yard dash) and mirth provoking (three-legged races, pie-eating spectacles), entertained participants and spectators alike.

"Fourth of July parade, Helena, Montana." Vintage photo postcard marked "M. Rieder, Publ." Mailed Helena, Montana, July 10, 1908.

Vintage embossed postcard marked "No. 51668."
Mailed Worcester, Massachusetts, July 1, 1909.

4th of JULY at Mendon
PROGRAM
One Hundred Guns at Sunrise.

Ball Game......................9:30 a. m.
Trap Shoot........................11 a. m.
Hundred Yard Dash............1:00 p. m.
Wheelbarrow Race.............1:30 p. m.
Potato Race.....................1:45 p. m.
Sack Race........................2:00 p. m.
Madam Marantette, 2:15 to 3:15......
.............................Society Horses
Ball Game........................3:30 p. m.
Tub Race.........................4:00 p. m.
Madam Marantette, Trotting Ostrich.,
.................................5:00 p. m.
Balloon Ascension and Triple Parachute
Drop.
Madam Marantette, High Jumping
Horses ....7:30 p. m.
One Hundred Dollars worth of Fireworks.
Plenty of Music all Day.
Moving Pictures at the Lyric afternoon and
evening.
Bowery Dance all day and evening.
For concessions apply to Geo. White, Men-
don, Mich.

5½" x 3½" program for July Fourth festivities
held in Mendon, Michigan.

The staging of patriotic tableaux, or "living pictures," taught the little ones about the past as they physically acted out scenes of historical significance. *The Designer* (1912), for example, suggested that participants portray scenes of the signing of the Declaration of Independence, the Goddess of Liberty, the Old Continentals, Yankee Doodle, the Angel of Peace, and/or Paul Revere's Ride. The following year, the magazine opted for pageants, plays, and drills:

> Children might perform on the lawn in . . . a pretty pageant or play about "The Progress of the Liberty Bell." Important events that have transpired since the Liberty Bell first proclaimed its message through the land could be represented in a series of tableaux. This could be followed by a comic feature—a Firecracker Drill, where small boys costumed as firecrackers go through a lively march and dance.

Abundant material for patriotic recitations, drills, songs, and short plays could be found in the small soft-cover books produced by educational publishers T.S Denison & Company of Chicago, Paine Publishing of Dayton, Ohio, and others.

Especially noteworthy were the creative approaches to "New Fourth" planning exemplified by group "theatre," as in stadium-staged renditions of "living flags," or enticing incentives like the then-princely fifty-cent "reward" offered to the boys and girls of Kintnersville, Pennsylvania, who refrained from handling fireworks of any type. And where private donations had once been the primary source of Independence Day funding, towns and cities increasingly stepped up to foot a portion of the bill.

The children themselves even came up with more personal attempts to reinforce fireworks reform. When suggestions for celebrating the Fourth appeared on the "Children's Hour" page of *The Housekeeper* (1904), fifteen-year-old Cecil Stults wrote:

> I think we could celebrate the Fourth with the good old picnics we love so well. The program and music are always the best part of a celebration. They could be made more elaborate to make up for lost features. The children would take a large part in the program. Of course, the Declaration of Independence is always read. What would a Fourth of July

celebration be without it? And above all, the dear old "Stars and Stripes" should be displayed everywhere. The sight of it is enough to arouse the spirit of patriotism in one's soul.

The same article included recollections from twelve-year-old Virginia Mayes on an especially memorable Fourth of July picnic.

I think there are many ways in which to spend "the glorious Fourth" besides shooting off fireworks all day. The custom in the little town of Princeton, Ky., could not have been more pleasantly spent . . . the children would all gather at the appointed meeting place, where were waiting large hay wagons, on which [they] piled with much fun and laughter. The mamas and papas came along in carriages and vehicles of every kind; and bringing up the rear, was the most important wagon of all, the one which carried the baskets full of good things to eat. The long procession drove through town amid the waving of flags and shouts of the children and, after arriving into the country for about three miles, at last stopped in a shady grove on the banks of a beautiful creek.

The young writer proceeded to describe how the children played in a nearby creek, picked wildflowers, and quenched their thirsts from big barrels of lemonade until it was time to feast on fried chicken.

"Oh that dinner!" she enthused, "It makes my mouth to think of it now!"

Yes, Virginia, it would appear that communities did know how to spend a safe and utterly entertaining "New Fourth" once upon an old-fashioned time!

HOW OUR TOWN SPENT THE FOURTH OF JULY

* **Chicago Heights, Illinois.** "In commemoration of the Declaration of Independence, we ask you to help us celebrate the day we were made a land of the free by noble men who pledged their lives, their fortunes, and their sacred honor, and we want everyone to join us in an old-fashioned Fourth of July celebration . . . [with a] parade, flags, bunting,

Vintage embossed postcard marked "Copyright 1908, P. Sander N.Y." Mailed Manitou, Oklahoma, June 28, 1909.

THE BABY PARADE ON THE MARCH AND LINED UP

Youngsters line up for the children's parade on Deerfield Street, Hartford, Connecticut (from "A Sensible Fourth of July," The Ladies' World, July 1908).

speaking, baseball, balloon ascensions, fireworks, and dancing. The old-fashioned is best after all. Everyone is cordially invited to take part in the parade . . . beginning at 10 o'clock." (*The Chicago Heights Star,* June 24, 1909)

* **Hartford, Connecticut.** "The programme begins at nine in the morning. While fathers and sons are decorating the exteriors of houses, mothers and daughters arrange the baby parade, and all the little people on the street march in gala costume. They carry baskets of flowers, Japanese paper kites and parasols and flags of various nations.

"At half-past ten the games begin. These have been arranged for all ages, and permission has been given by the park association for them to be placed on the open lawns and watched from the cool shadows of the trees along the sides. Many of the ladies on the street keep open-house and welcome all visitors, and serve afternoon tea, iced lemonade and light refreshments.

"[At night] the men and boys light the candles in the myriad of Japanese lanterns. It is then that the fete is at its best and the street looks like a fairyland. Under arches of

RED, WHITE AND BLUE GOODS

Patriotic occasions are celebrated very often with parades of decorated automobiles, baby carriages, etc. Whole costumes are made of paper as shown in the lower right hand picture or effective regalia may consist of crepe paper hats and sashes made from Streamers, No. P23.

Banners for parades and for school exercises are inexpensive if made from crepe paper. The variety of colors is exceptional and the work may be done by the children themselves. Parades are always greatly enjoyed by young people.

Patriotic snapshots (Dennison's 1916 Gala Book).

Assorted late-nineteenth/early-twentieth-century Fourth of July celebration ribbons.

bunting, on a small impromptu grand stand, the town band plays a concert. During this the Committee of Fireworks keeps up a continuous display. Afterward the young people have confetti battles and burn sparklers. Though [the people] have celebrated in a most patriotic and very pretty way, they have also managed to retain their own fingers and the eyesight of their children, and have not even had their homes burned over their heads." (*The Ladies' World*, July 1908)

* **Momence, Illinois.** "Grand celebration Monday, July 5, 1909. The beautiful new Soldiers' Monument erected by the Woman's Relief Corps. will be unveiled and dedicated, the address to be given by [the governor]. A good program of athletic sports will be held, dancing, big civic parade, good music." (*The Chicago Heights Star*, June 24, 1909) *NOTE: Independence Day celebrations of this era were usually held on Monday whenever the holiday fell on Sunday.*

* **Portland, Oregon.** "Cash prizes were promised for the best-decorated home, store, public building, carriage, automobile, etc. Everybody contributed. Some job printers distributed facsimiles of the Declaration of Independence; a hardware store gave a bell; a piano house, sheet-music; and so on through a long list. Trumpets, bunting, ribbons, hatbands, flags, badges, etc., were offered freely.

"To remind us of those first heroic peals of long ago, from early morning until late at night all bells were ringing. Every man, woman and child wore our national colors in some forms. The children carried horns and drums, and used them too! Every vehicle of any sort bore the colors in flags, flowers or bunting. Street-car and railroad companies vied with each other in making their cars attractive. From every building waved our national colors. On hundreds of lawns flagpoles had seemingly sprung up in a night.

"There was a grand parade in the forenoon, in which all things were in keeping with the day. In the afternoon our patriotism was expressed in sweet tones, either singly or in concord. Bands played, trumpets sounded, instruments of all kinds were heard. There was music in the streets, in the homes, in the parks—everywhere.

"The crowning glory of it all came where waved our flag

before, now shone forth red, white and blue lights. Where electric lights were available the spirit of competition led to great display. Homes and buildings were illuminated. Lawns of both great and small dimensions added their quota of fancy lanterns; the parks were veritable fairylands. Best of all, in almost every gathering during the day the national airs were sung; and even where there was not musical accompaniment the voices rang strong and true." (*The Ladies' Home Journal,* June 1907)

* **In a small Western town.** "[The] pageant was, from all accounts, a great success. There was Paul Revere on a Shetland pony, and a host of worthies acting their parts to life. After the parade, there was ice cream and lemonade and various jollifications." (*The New York Times,* June 25, 1911)

* **Harvey, Illinois.** "Fine shade, grand music, most eloquent speakers in the state. Races! Races! Races! Ball games, climbing the greased pole, fireworks let off from a stand in front of the city calaboose." (*The Harvey Tribune-Citizen,* July 5, 1912)

* **Cincinnati, Ohio.** "Cincinnati is to have its first 'safe and sane' celebration. . . . No prohibition has been placed on legitimate fireworks, but cannon crackers, harmful torpedoes, toy cannons, blank cartridges, giant caps and similar dangerous explosives are barred.

"To console the children for the loss of these dangerous playthings, [the Fourth of July Carnival Association] has arranged a series of patriotic exercises and amusements covering the entire day.

"Starting at 9:30 there will be exercises in twenty school yards, and at the same hour six hundred children will form the 'Musical Flag' on Government Square and go through a long programme of songs. In the afternoon all the city playgrounds will be filled with children, marching, singing and playing. In the evening the programme

Fourth of July Celebration at Fleischmann's N.Y.

"*Fourth of July Celebration at Fleischmann's N.Y.*" *Vintage photo postcard marked "Albert Hahn No. 819." Postally unusued.*

provides band concerts and fireworks exploded by officials of the association." (*The New York Times*, July 3, 1911)

* **Richmond Hill, Long Island, New York.** "The morning of the Fourth was spent in decorating the houses with American flags of every size, bunting and Japanese lanterns. At dark all the lanterns were lit, making the street a myriad of fantastic colors . . . the street was roped off to guard against [anyone] getting too close to the fireworks. A band of ten pieces played during the fireworks intermissions and young people made to dance on cement sidewalks and grassy green lawns. The fireworks lasted about two hours . . . [more] dancing [continued] until eleven o'clock. Pleasant good-nights were exchanged as the decorations were taken down." (*The Ladies' World*, July 1913)

Vintage embossed postcard marked "International Art Publ. Co., Series No. 4398." Postally unused with handwritten salutations on reverse.

* **Chicago, Illinois.** "Chicago celebrated its second sane Fourth of July to-day with a parade, historical tableaux, patriotic exercises, play festivals, and band concerts in the public parks. The programme began with a patriotic pageant, three miles in length, composed of 5,000 men, women and children, and twenty elaborate floats depicting events in the city's history. Seventeen nationalities were represented in the parade . . . three hundred thousand people watched the procession in the downtown streets." (*The New York Times*, July 5, 1911)

* **In a North Carolina town.** "Last year the feature of the day was a parade of more than a hundred floats, carriages and automobiles. It was a dazzling spectacle, as clubs, societies, business firms and individuals all did their best to make the day memorable. Everywhere in the procession there were flags . . . then there was an oration, followed by a dinner; a parade of firemen, with sports, in the afternoon; and in the evening a lawn party and band concert. Everybody was contented." (*The Ladies' Home Journal*, June 1907)

* **Roebling, New Jersey.** "Setting the example for a safe and sane

Fourth of July, Roebling . . . is to have a model Independence Day celebration. Plans announced to-day for the biggest and liveliest in the brief history of the town [include] a flag-raising, parade, athletic contest, band concert, and a fireworks display." (*The New York Times*, July 3, 1909)

* **Homewood, Illinois.** "The big parade will form at the east end of town at 12 o'clock noon. One feature of the parade will be the beautiful floats now in course of construction. The [sponsoring] East End Citizens' Association will enter a peace float while other floats will be entered by all the lodges and churches and the businessmen's association. The Ravisloe club will enter three flower floats.

"An important feature of the day's program will be a ball game between Homewood and Chicago Heights, both uniform teams. Vaudeville shows will help you forget your troubles. There will be dancing in the large pavilion and many other attractions.

"The Auburn cadets will be on hand and give exhibition drills and anyone who has not seen these boys drill should take advantage of this opportunity. The T.O.S. of A. fife and drum corps has been engaged to lead the parade and furnish music on the ground.

"In the evening there will be a grand display of fireworks and you cannot spend a saner or safer Fourth of July than by going to Homewood, Monday July 5.

"We invite you to come, bring your lunch and spend the day. Ample provision will be made for those who wish to purchase their lunch on the grounds." (*The Harvey Tribune*, July 2, 1915)

* **New York City, New York.** "For several years past the residents of Decatur Street, from Ralph to Howard Avenue, have contributed a liberal sum for fireworks and other forms of entertainment, and the Fourth this year was celebrated

Children with flags and tricolor admiral party hats ca. 1919. Vintage photograph.

with quite as much fervor and patriotism as in the past. The block was filled with bunting of all shapes and sizes, and this, with music and fireworks and refreshments, gave the contributors a busy day. The celebration was enjoyed by several hundred persons who live outside the block." (*The New York Times*, July 6, 1897)

* **Council Bluffs, Iowa.** "A squad of twenty-five little boys and girls will be ceremoniously sworn in as special policemen to-morrow morning by Chief Richmond, and detailed to duty as a fireworks squad. A badge certifying to the bearers' official standing will be pinned on each little blouse, and the youngsters thus distinguished will go forth to see that there is no premature celebration of the glorious Fourth. Their function also will be to see that other children are not tempted by the fact of possession into using explosives of a known dangerous nature on the great day." (*The New York Times*, July 1, 1907)

* **Denver, Colorado.** "The playground children were busy for a week before the Fourth last year making kites and practicing flying them in preparation for the kite tournament. Any one under 18 could compete, the only condition being that he make his own kite. Prizes were awarded for the kite that flew the highest, for the most beautiful kite, the kite most original in its design, for a patriotic kite, for a model airplane and for the winner in the kite fight." (*The Designer*, July 1915)

* **In a city in Texas.** "Since it was too warm to plan for much in the daytime, [it was] arranged for five hundred children to march in the early evening. Clad in white, with tricolored bands draped over their shoulders, each carried garlands of bright flowers. On the schoolground these garlands were used Maypole effect, an American flag floating above. There was a hush as a man clad in Colonial costume . . . read the Declaration of Independence. Then came singing, tableaux, stirring music played by a band, while

Vintage postcard with embossed edges marked "Fourth of July Series No. 9." Postally unused.

the children marched by, each carrying a representation of the Liberty Bell, and formed a 'living flag.'" (*The Ladies' Home Journal,* June 1907)

* **Harvey, Illinois.** "The parade will start promptly at 10 o'clock. Immediately afterward, the [crowd will be addressed] by Edward F. Trefz, who is field secretary of the Chambers of Commerce of the United States and [reputed] to be one of the best orators in the country.

"The greatest array of games and sports ever had in this vicinity will take up the time in the afternoon beginning at 1 o'clock . . . [some of] the prizes offered to winners are as follows:

* Boys race, under 12 years. 1st prize, pair roller skates; 2nd, bow and arrow.
* Boys race, under 16 years. 1st, pair $3.50 shoes; 2nd, pocket knife.
* Mile race, open. 1st, pair outing trousers; 2nd, $2 shirt.
* Quarter mile, open. 1st, fountain pen; 2nd, $2 shirt.
* Forty yard race for girls under 12 years. 1st, bottle perfume; 2nd, box candy.
* Fifty yard race for girls under 16 years. 1st, $3 in merchandise; 2nd, tennis racket.
* Ladies race, open. 1st, $3 umbrella; 2nd, pair white kid gloves.
* Married ladies race. 1st, porch chair; 2nd, Hot Point electric iron.
* Sack race. Order for $2.50 in cleaning.
* Three-legged race. 1st, box cigars; 2nd, box cigars.
* Barrel race. Shirt.

"The volunteer firemen will give an exhibition run against time, laying hose and attaching nozzle. This is the team which expects to take some prizes at the state fireman's tournament." (*The Harvey Tribune,* July 2, 1915)

Keep These Little Hints in Mind When You Make Your Fourth of July Plans

Excerpted from *The Ladies' Home Journal,* June 1907

Bonfires	Living Flags	Burlesque Features
Floral Fetes	Bell Ringing	Moving Pictures
Bugle Calls	Archery Contests	Torchlight Parades

Enact the signing of the Declaration.

If there are chimes, have "America" played.

Keep piano-music going all over town.

Fifers and drummers to march in Continental costume.

Print patriotic songs on cards for free distribution; sing these songs at band concerts.

Have strings of lanterns across the streets.

Let boys have a camp-fire and cook their own dinner.

Send up small balloons with "reward" post-cards attached.

Have the little ones give an entertainment on the porch.

Exhibit war relics in the town hall: swords, flags, pictures, letters, etc.

At the sunrise flag-raising have a lot of little flags rolled up to drop out of the big one.

Wherever there is water have a water fete: decorated canoes; swimming matches; bridge and raft illuminations.

About town have banners bearing such inscriptions as: "Give me liberty or give me death;" "Liberty and union, now and forever;" "Proclaim liberty throughout all the land, unto all the inhabitants thereof."

I LOVE A PARADE

A Photo Album

"The parade should be one in which the life of the town shall be expressed, not only the commercial life, but all life. First, the mayor and the council or commission, and all the city employees, from elected officers to appointed janitors; then the city teams and horses, with prizes for the best-decorated wagons and the best cared-for horses; the Fire Department, with its engines, hose-cart and other apparatus; the Water Department, with its sprinkling-carts; the telephone and telegraph companies; the Post Office, with all the carriers marching in uniform. Next, the farmers' wagons and horses, with prizes again; floats of the business houses; and floats of the different schools, with all the children marching."

McCall's Magazine, July 1913

Decorated car with overhead figure of the Statue of Liberty being pulled by patriotically decorated eagle. Vintage photograph ca. 1920 stamped "Photo by Harvey Patteson Service Engraving Co., San Antonio, Tex."

Uncle Sam and Miss Liberty head a horse-drawn parade float with patriotic group ca. 1910. Vintage real-photo postcard. Postally unused.

Patriotic bicycle as parade float ca. 1915. Vintage real-photo postcard with handwritten endorsement "Morris Hecox & son Robert." Postally unused.

Oversized decorated Simplex coaster wagon parade float. Vintage photograph; words "July 4, 1926. Dorothy–13. Henry–11." endorsed on reverse.

Pint-sized Miss Columbia and Uncle Sam. Vintage photograph ca. 1910 stamped "K&E Photo-Kraft."

Decorated horse-drawn cartridge. Vintage photograph ca. 1915.

FIREWORKS FEVER

"Among the novelties this year are Roman candles with a repertoire of tumbling feats. They perform acrobatic stunts in mid-heaven, and throw a series of somersaults. Another kind will imitate lightning. As the stars ascend they will emit a series of dazzling flashes. For a new type of bomb a score of great spiders will shoot out and will seem to chase each other far aloft . . . There'll be plenty of noise anyhow and a new sound is to be added to the bangs of the old-time fireworks. Rockets, Roman candles and St. Catherine wheels will whistle as they go off. Noise is what the people want."

The New York Times, June 25, 1907

Displays of fireworks probably constitute the most thrilling—if not the most beloved—custom associated with celebrating the Fourth of July. The use, and occasional to frequent misuse, of fireworks in America date back to colonial times—notably, in 1731 the colony of Rhode Island enacted laws calling for substantial fines to be levied against "any person [who] fires any gun, pistol, rocket, squibs or other fire-works, in any road, street, lane or tavern or other public house, after sunsetting and before sunrising."

Fireworks were on display when America was declared an independent nation and have cast their glittering magic on the night air with each anniversary that followed. Over the course of the 1800s, however, the ruckus caused by ever more powerful and dangerous types of noisemakers "made the night hideous" for ordinary citizens. "Somehow the production of noise has come to be insisted on upon this particular anniversary as a patriotic duty and the only homage to its greatness," *The New York Times* wrote in 1873. "When or how the custom first became established, no historian . . . has informed us."

By the turn-of-the-twentieth-century, the popular explosive devices became the subject of intensive safety concerns that ultimately led to an ever-expanding variety of laws meant to regulate their use. Be they large or small, civically sponsored or backyard variety, relatively "safe" or outright dangerous, fireworks are an essential part of the Independence Day equation. And so, without further ado . . . *on with the show!*

FIREWORKS GLOSSARY

* Cap cane: long wooden device with a metal tip that fires a cap upon impact.

* Cannon cracker: massive firecracker of up to fourteen inches in length.

* Catherine wheel or pinwheel: center spike-mounted spiral tube that produces colorful flames and sparks as it spins rapidly.

* Chaser: firework that whistles across the ground.

* Daylight firework: pyrotechnic device that produces smoke, noise, or other novelty effects in lieu of light.

* Fire balloon: open-bottomed paper lantern of a smaller size (but up to six feet) that drifts upward when inflated by warm air.

* Fountain: cone-shaped firework that discharges a shower of sparks.

* Ladyfinger: tiny firecracker approximately three-quarter-inch long.

* Mandarin string: length of tiny interconnected firecrackers that can be hung from above and detonated as a single ear-popping unit.

* Rocket or skyrocket: cone-topped cylinder attached to a wooden rod that leaves a trail of glowing sparks when shot into the sky.

* Roman candle: long paper tube that shoots out small stars one at a time.

* Set piece: ground-level framework fitted with fireworks designed to produce a fiery image or motto, either stationary or animated.

* Spinner: firework that spins and produces noise as it rises a small distance from the ground.

* Squib: homemade firecracker.

* Torpedo: gravel-filled sachet-style impact firecracker that explodes when stepped on or thrown to the ground.

Vintage embossed postcard marked "Fourth of July Series No. 4." Mailed Pleasant City, Ohio, July 6, 1911.

Vintage postcard marked "Copyrighted 1906 by Blanchard, Young & Co., Providence." Postally unused.

Vintage embossed postcard marked "P. Sander 440." Mailed Worcester, Massachusetts, July 3, 1910.

* Toy cannon: small but hefty cannon made to propel firecrackers and/or other projectiles.

* Toy pistol: flimsily constructed gun designed to fire either blank cartridges or caps.

YES, WE HAVE FIREWORKS

* *Best Sellers.* "A tour among the fireworks dealers developed the fact that, while the strictly noise producing contrivances are not going quite as fast as usual, the sale of fireworks in general is by far larger this year than for many years past. . . . The orders are coming in from every quarter for colored lights, Roman candles, rockets, rainbow wheels, jeweled jets, pyric cascades, and innumerable other contrivances for patriotic illuminations, and it is predicted that on tomorrow night the sky from every point of view in New York will be a flower garden in green, yellow, blue, purple, and red." (*The New York Times*, July 3, 1901)

* *Quiet Please!* "The Red Cross Committee is most appreciated by the sick or invalids to whom it is almost a necessity that the day be a quiet one. This committee . . . sends out its members to find out the houses where sickness is. The day before the Fourth the doors of the households that desire it are marked with cards bearing a red cross. The adults in that neighborhood are then asked to keep the children as quiet as possible and not to celebrate in the vicinity." (*The Ladies' Home Journal*, June 1908)

* *Fireworks in Plenty.* "All the improvements . . . have been made in the aerial pieces. Some of the effects given in midair from one piece are so elaborate that it looks as if they were being set off above by some unseen hand. There are willowtree rockets which cover acres of space when they burst, spreading and drooping until they reach the ground; the electric shower and telescope rockets, which give fine effects. Some pretty little fireworks for the children are the silver geysers, electric lights which show crimson and electric fire, and trolley wheels. These are each one cent, and last year were two. The five-cent Ferris wheel is absolutely new this year." (*The New York Times*, June 14, 1895)

Civic Fireworks Tonight!

- "*Illuminated Shield.*
- "*Man in the Moon.* A gorgeous full moon, with a laughing face and twinkling eyes, illuminated with brilliant colored fires, changing to scintillating showers which form a halo of golden rays about the moon.
- "*Liberty Emblem.*
- "*Bust of Washington.* A beautiful portrait of Washington, illuminated in all the colors of the rainbow, surrounded by brilliant sun cases, displaying sparkling fires, and terminating with artillery salutes.
- "*Comet's Frolic.*
- "*Polka Battery.* A combination of illuminated wheels, large battery fountains and brilliant circles of golden fires, with crimson and emerald centres, while on sides are displayed jets of variegated stars and streamers.
- "*Daisy Wheel.*
- "*Gallopade.* Within a magnificent circle, revolving with great rapidity and discharging in every direction streams of brilliant and sparkling fires, are displayed two gorgeous Saxon wheels revolving in opposite directions and charged with sun fires.
- "*Monitor Battery.* A grand battery of colored stars and variegated meteors thrown to heights of 200 feet, making a magnificent aerial display.
- "*Chaplet of Roses.* A beautiful hexagon wheel, the base revolving with emerald and crimson centers, above which is displayed a bouquet of roses in rainbow tints."

(Original "4th of July Program"–Union City, Pennsylvania, July 4, 1901)

* *Like the Usual Holiday–Plenty of Noise.* "The order . . . prohibiting the use of pistols, cannon, and firecrackers by the small boy and large man of New-York in celebration of Independence Day was treated with about as much attention

Fireworks for July 4th at Factory Prices. Full-page vintage ad placed by the Masten & Wells Fireworks Manufacturing Company in the June 1893 issue of Century Magazine.

Box of early twentieth-century No. 10 American Beauty sparklers marked "Superb HALCO Brand." 10" x 1¾".

Vintage embossed postcard marked "Copyright 1907 by Suhling & Koenn Co." Mailed Geneva, Nebraska, July 2, 1908.

yesterday as such orders generally receive. [The] night was made hideous by the explosion of all kinds of firearms and crackers. After midnight the din was simply terrific, and the popping of firecrackers and the snap of torpedoes and toy pistols made nervous people start and jump aside quickly as they walked the streets in the early morning. The small boy was abroad in force, and the sidewalks were strewn with smoking fragments of crackers and torpedo papers. In the matter of noise, yesterday's celebration showed no falling off in enthusiasm from those of former years and something of an increase over those of the last two or three years." (*The New York Times*, July 5, 1885)

* *Bandages OUT, Ice Cream IN.* "The children have forgotten all about the deadly explosives in their glee over the athletic contests. Two experts have been engaged to handle the big fireworks display in the evening so that everybody may enjoy the fun without the risk of burned fingers or scorched eyebrows. As a result of the plans the local drug store has cut its annual order of bandages and arnica and stocked up on ice cream sodas instead." (*The New York Times*, July 3, 1909)

* *Smart sales pitch.* "FIREWORKS [The Sane Kind]: The fates and Governor Deneen have decreed that we celebrate Independence Day in a sane and conservative manner. We have stocked up with goods that come within the law, and have an abundance of everything of a harmless character, such as Chinese Crackers, Cap Pistols, Cap Canes, Cap Cannons, Pin Wheels, Rockets, Candles, Snakes, Sparklers and many other novelties which will amuse and delight the youngsters. Also a large variety of Night Works, Balloons, Airships, and Colored Fire." (Display ad, Ritter's Candy Store—*The Chicago Heights Star*, June 29, 1911)

* *He Prefers a Noisy Day.* "Independence Day brought a double celebration to Joshua Zeltlein yesterday at the home of his son-in-law [where] he celebrated his 106th birthday. Mr. Zeitlein said he preferred a noisy Fourth of July to

the much agitated 'safe and sane' Fourth [and expressed] the belief that he would live a good many more years. He smokes a pipe every day and indulges moderately in whisky and beer." (*The New York Times*, July 5, 1910)

* *Fireworks Makers Hard Hit by Sales Ban.* "'The Mayor's order will have a most serious effect,' said Henry J. Pain, Vice President of the Pain Fireworks Manufacturing Company. 'It will kill the trade. What ought to have been done would have been for the Aldermen to have passed a sweeping ordinance against firecrackers over five inches long, toy pistols, dynamite, caps, blank cartridges, cane ammunition, salutes, or maroons. . . . A committee of fifty experts representing all the States should be convened and should draw up some such regulation for this country founded on their experience. But harmless fireworks should always stay a part of Fourth of July as long as we sing, *The rocket's red glare, bombs bursting in the air.*'" (*The New York Times*, April 3, 1910)

* *Excitement in the Fireworks Stores.* "Nothing but the toy shops before Christmas equal the big fireworks establishments on the day before the Fourth. There are places in which the small boy, to whom the day is dedicated in these modern times, would revel if he had the opportunity. But he has not. To see firecrackers in quantities that fill what appear to be great straw-covered tea chests, and hundreds of those, with menageries of day fireworks, mortars, bombshells, and serpents, all lying around in the most bewildering profusion, presents a temptation to buy or plunder that is irresistible to the young and imaginative celebrator of the glorious Fourth.

"Their fathers and big brothers are there in crowds and carry away bundles nearly as large as themselves. Occasionally a mother comes in and lays down a big handful of sweet-smelling roses to make a purchase, but she is one in a hundred, for to the mothers the day is not one of unalloyed joy.

"If the mother is interested in picturesque nomenclature, she cannot fail to be pleased with the varied stock on hand in one of these shops. There are prismatic whirl-winds, batteries of stars, aerial contortionists, surprise boxes, umbrellas of fire, floral fountains of golden spray; flower pots, with handles, colored

Vintage postcard marked "331 F.A. Owen Publishing Co." Postally unused.

Vintage embossed postcard marked "P. Sander 440." Mailed Humboldt, Michigan, July 3, 1912.

Ye spit-devil is a wily beast
That comes but once a year,
And wriggle about maiden's ankles
On mischief bent, I fear.

*Vintage embossed postcard marked "Fourth of July Series No. 1."
Postally unused.*

rosettes and geysers, gas wells and colored show bills, volcanoes, bombette fountains, Jacks in boxes, to say nothing of Pharaoh's serpent's eggs, snake's nests, snakes in the grass, beehives, yellow-jackets, and grasshoppers." (*The New York Times,* July 4, 1894)

* *Fireworks Notice.* "The attention of the public is called to the city ordinance concerning fireworks, including the following: the discharge, firing or use of all firecrackers, rockets, torpedoes, Roman candles, or other fireworks or substances designed and intended for pyrotechnic display, and of all pistols, canes, cannons or other appliances, using blank cartridges or caps . . . is hereby prohibited. Provided that the mayor may permit the public display of fireworks by properly qualified individuals under the direct supervision of experts in the handling of fireworks. Provided also that such display[s] shall be of such a character and so located, discharged or fired as, in the opinion of the chief of the fire department, shall not be hazardous to surrounding property or endanger any persons. This, as well as all other regulations of the ordinance, will be strictly enforced. L.H. Hook, Mayor." (Public notice—*The Chicago Heights Star,* July 2, 1914)

* *Mrs. Smith's Grievances.* "While the festive youth of Carlisle Street were expressing their patriotism in the discharge of firecrackers on July 4, a big cracker, or bomb, found its way underneath the robes of Mrs. Caroline Smith. It there exploded, causing Mrs. Smith to make an involuntary ascent into the air, and setting fire to her clothing. She charged Charles Flink, whose home was opposite hers, with having thrown the bomb to annoy and harm her . . . and then began a civil suit against him in the City Court, asking for $1,000 damages." (*The New York Times,* July 25, 1884)

* *Some Advice for the Fourth.*
"Don't throw lighted firecrackers above your head, especially if there are little girls with light dresses standing near you.
"Don't hold powder and lighted punk in the same hand.

"Don't look into the mouth of a toy cannon to see why it hasn't gone off.

"Don't put firecrackers into your pockets.

"Don't drop a roman candle if a spark happens to burn you. Be brave, and shake it all the harder, but never drop it, for the balls may do serious damage.

"Don't leave matches and lighted punk where ladies may tread on them.

"Don't fool with toy pistols.

"Don't make fun of the little ones who take pleasure in torpedoes and are afraid of firecrackers. You were little once, remember.

"Don't get cross because mother or the servant tells you that you are wasting matches or scattering them about.

"Don't be mean, but let the ragged boys and girls pick up some crackers which may not go off. You might drop some on purpose for them, if you wished to be generous." (*The New York Times,* July 1, 1894)

* From Ahhh to OUCH! "The Fourth and fireworks are synonymous with the small boy and fatalities. Very often the small sister is included among the patriotic victims of a great day. The wise mother, recognizing the fascinating fun of fireworks to the small folk, begins early to guard against the fatalities without handicapping the fun.

"First, in regard to matches, she insists that the firecrackers be lighted with punk, not only from an economical standpoint, but for safety as well. By using the punk, close contact is avoided with firecracker fuses.

"Second, she instructs children not to stand directly in front of the firecracker while lighting it, but to stand at one side. Neither will she allow firecrackers placed under tin vessels.

"The wise mother knows that one should be prepared for Fourth-of-July emergencies—that it is not enough to know what to do, but how to do it as well. She provides herself with a package of absorbent cotton or lint, a bandage roll and court plaster." (*The Delineator,* July 1908)

Vintage embossed postcard marked "PFB Series No. 9507." Postally ususued with message penciled on reverse.

Vintage embossed postcard marked "I.P.C." Postally unused.

Fireworks Is Wonder of All

The New-Castle (Pennsylvania) Tribune, July 5, 1910

Vintage postcard marked "332." Mailed Saint Paul, Minnesota, July 6, 1909.

Dazzling in its brilliancy and surpassing in its splendor anything ever before seen in New Castle, the display of fireworks on Boyles field was easily the crowning feature of the big Fourth.

More than 20,000 people stood in awe while the set pieces flamed in all the colors of the rainbow, while the rockets flew like meteors to the sky, and while the bursting bombs shook the very firmament and woke a thousand echoes in the surrounding hills and valleys.

Beneath the glow of the searchlight bombs whose brilliancy rivaled the splendor of the midday sun, the human sea of upturned faces formed a picture that no language can describe, nor artist paint. It was one of those grand spectacles that must be seen to be appreciated—that cannot be separated from the emotion it inspires.

Although the display of fireworks was not scheduled to begin till 9 o'clock, the crowd began collecting before night. Many came in automobiles and carriages. Scores carried camp stools and chairs. The Boyles field never before held such a crowd; it is doubtful if it ever will again.

From the moment from the first set piece glowed its "welcome" till the words of fire said "Good Night," the display was fast and furious. And as some particularly brilliant feature pleased the crowd a long drawn "O-h" from thousands at once showed the admiration of the crowd.

Following the blazing "welcome," the next set piece was a huge American eagle in many colors. The crowd cheered lustily as the national emblem lighted up the scene.

Another patriotic emblem which pleased the crowd was a big star seven feet across which changed colors rapidly as it burned.

Some of the other set pieces included the following: Search light wheel, 20 feet across, with seven wheels revolving in almost as many colors; two snakes fighting; American rose, revolving, 12 feet across.

Niagara Falls, 25 feet high and nearly 10 feet across. This was a particularly fine feature, the water being represented by sparks and a sort of fire.

Another piece was called the bombardment and it was certainly true to name for it sounded like a hundred cannons going off in rapid succession.

The Electric Foundation, 20 feet high, was considered by Fazzoni Bros., the manufacturers, to be their masterpiece. It contained all the colors of the rainbow and brought forth loud exclamations of delight. There were many other features among the set pieces that were as novel as they were pretty.

While the set pieces were beautiful it seemed to be the shells and rockets that called forth the greatest admiration. Probably this was because they could be seen to better advantage.

The one great feature of the aerial exhibition that awakened more astonishment than anything else was the searchlight bombs. These were sent up like an ordinary rocket. When they burst there was released a ball of fire that made the electric arc lights look like tallow candles. Though the balls of fire did not appear to be more than two or three inches in diameter, they lighted up the entire field so brilliantly that you could see to read a newspaper anywhere. Some of the bombs had two balls of fire. A peculiar feature of these balls was that they seemed to have an attraction for each other. They soared off in the same direction, keeping closely together, but revolving about each other. Other but subsequent bombs showed that they were not as some of them floated six or seven feet apart. Not only were these stars the most brilliant of any released, but they were also long lived, floating several hundred feet before going out.

Among these shells the "searchlight" were probably the loudest, although all of the reports were loud enough to be

Vintage embossed postcard marked "Fourth of July Series No. 2." Mailed Xenia, Ohio, July 4, 1912.

Vintage embossed postcard marked "Fourth of July Series No. 2." Mailed Philadelphia, Pennsylvania, July 2, 1913.

May you always be satisfied with the proudest title a man can wear AN AMERICAN CITIZEN.

heard for many miles. The air seemed to be just right for the shells to make their best detonations. One could hear the echoes and reverberations in all directions.

Among some of the shells that received the loudest applause may be mentioned: the national shells, red, white and blue; jeweled mine shells, Cascade shells, revolving in mid-air, showing a representation of Niagara Falls; willow tree shells. These shot to a great height and on bursting took the form of a willow tree with long, hanging branches of sparks gradually spreading until they reached the ground.

The peacock plume shells, displaying a broad swelling spread of liquid gold streams of glittering radiance, with feathery edges gradually spreading and dissolving in a cloud of sparkling mist, were greatly admired.

The dragon shells caused a shudder through the crowd, as the hissing, fiery serpents zigzagged through the heavens. Closely allied to them were the prismatic bomb shells. These bombs, after reaching a great altitude, discharged parachutes, each carrying a pin wheel attached. While sailing in the air the pin wheels revolved, making a very pretty effect.

Some of the other shells were as follows: Willow tree shells with a whistle and falling in the form of a ship and spreading until they reached the ground; shells exploding in the air and each shell giving out a battery shooting many times; shells of all colors, such as yellow, green, orange, red, white, blue and purple.

Among the rockets were the following: Shooting star rockets, electric shower rockets, parachute rockets, cascade rockets, diamond chain rockets, shooting rockets, all discharging at the same time, representing falling stars; rockets representing a peacock plume with feathery edges as they fall to the earth.

The fireworks were manufactured by Fazzoni Bros. of New Castle. They were ample evidence that the manufacturers understand their business. Not only was the display magnificent but it was put off in a way that pleased the crowd. There were no long waits between acts. There was something doing all the time. The fireworks on the Boyles field, July 4, 1910 will go down in history as one of the big events New Castle's best celebration.

Vintage postcard. Postally unused.

HOW INVITING!

"The very words 'Fourth of July' suggest a party. Every true American feels a desire in his heart to celebrate this occasion in a fitting way . . . [and] the invitations, of course, are most important."

The Designer, July 1914

Hostesses in the late nineteenth and early twentieth centuries *loved* to entertain with considerable panache and routinely lavished their guests with the sort of elegant soup-to-nuts thoroughness that was a hallmark of the era. Parties planned for the Fourth of July, even those for less formal occasions like picnics, still demanded creativeness on the part of the hostess when it came to invitations.

To that end, *The Designer* (1903) suggested that announcements be penned on small flags that had been decoratively edged with tiny firecrackers; surprisingly, the normally detailed-oriented editors neglected to mention whether the cracker attachments were meant to be strictly decorative or, given the pyrotechnic-friendly attitudes of the era, the real thing! *(NOTE: Given that the 1942 Flag Code provides that, amongst other things, the American flag should neither be attached to any articles or costumes nor be depicted on items of a temporary or disposable nature, this particular use of the flag—as it was suggested, well in advance of the code being adopted, by a magazine editor who doubtless meant no disrespect—is reprinted herein* for historical interest. *Please revisit the preface of this book for comments pertaining to recounting the past.)*

Ever mindful of prevailing mores, though, many a party planner might have felt obliged to suppress her mirthful side in favor of more conventional protocols. As such, *The Designer* (1904) opted for advising hostesses to prepare invitations using their visiting cards: party specifics could be printed across the bottom of the card and it could be further embellished with a hand-painted watercolor rendition of the Stars and Stripes.

Editorial tastes at *McCall's Magazine* (1914), on the other hand, ran toward less fussy bronze-colored pasteboard Liberty bells tied with red, white, and blue baby ribbon. Formats aside, though, an invitation to a get-together on the Glorious Fourth was always a welcome sign of the merry day of food, frolic, and fun that lie ahead.

BE MY GUEST:
INSPIRATIONAL INVITATIONS

* "Write the invitations on pieces of fresh white tissue paper with a finely-pointed soft pencil. With the writing inside, carefully draw the papers over wads of white cotton batting, and twist them at the top so that they look like giant torpedoes. Paste the top of each with a slip bearing the name of the [invitee along with] the directions to 'open carefully.'" (*The Ladies' World*, July 1908)

* "Cut little drum-shapes out of heavy art paper, shading them in with penwork or water-color. Write the invitation in appropriate form. Something like this would excite curiosity and make the party interesting–'PATRIOTS: Drums will beat, and Congress will assemble on Independence Day at Hillview House at three o'clock of ye afternoon. You are heartily bidden to attend.'" (*The Designer*, July 1914)

Vintage embossed postcard marked "250." Mailed York, Pennsylvania, July 2, 1909.

* "The invitations are written on strips of paper about three inches wide, rolled up and wrapped with red tissue paper to resemble firecrackers. A bit of string at one end forms the fuse. Small sticks of candy are broken into even lengths and [placed inside]." (*Woman's Home Companion*, July 1915)

* "Invitations to the party are written upon tiny sheets of white note-paper in blue ink, and a wee paper flag in red,

white and blue, cut from a roll of crepe-paper is pasted at the top of each. The white envelopes which hold the invitations are addressed, as the invitations were, in blue ink and carry red stamps in the corner, and on the flap of each envelope is pasted a little flag seal." (*McCall's Magazine*, July 1913)

* "Liberty bell shapes cut from eggshell cardboard make interesting invitations. One side can be bronzed with paint which comes for the purpose, while on the reverse the invitation is written, in words of this sort: 'A Mass Meeting of American Patriots, past and present, assembled to celebrate our national birthday, will be held at the schoolhouse on July 4th at 2:30 P.M. All good patriots welcome.'" (*The Designer*, July 1915)

Decorative boxed paper accents by Dennison Mfg. Co. ca. 1910s-20s. Uncle Sam Patriotic Cut-Outs (4¼" x 1¾"), Uncle Sam Gummed Seals (2" square), American Flag Gummed Seals (3" x 2").

THREE CHEERS FOR THE RED, WHITE, AND BLUE DÉCOR

"Patriotism and Entertainment can well make their bow together on the Fourth of July, and Patriotism has many an historic garment and accessory of individuality with which to bedeck Hospitality, and make such an occasion attractive."

The Ladies' World, July 1903

"No entertainment throughout the year offers greater or more effective possibilities than a Fourth of July celebration," promised *Entertainments For All Seasons* (1904), and by all accounts, patriotic hostesses reveled in embellishing party venues—inside as well as out—with all things red, white, and blue. That quintessential arbiter of modes and manners, *The Ladies' Home Journal*, concurred.

With July comes the Fourth, always suggestive of the red, white and blue—bunting, flags and fireworks; and whatever kind of celebration is decided upon, whether boating, picnicking, or an "at-home" fete, the national emblem and colors must rule the day. The colors of no nation lend themselves so beautifully and so gracefully to decoration as do those of America, and in whatever fete given our national colors should in some manner take part.

Naturally enough, Fourth of July party planners were unanimous in their decision to use the American flag as the cornerstone of their holiday decorating plans. Period magazines advised decorators to drape archways with larger flags and use smaller ones "in every available space." Newel posts, door and window frames, and even dining tables could be made festive with diminutive versions of Old Glory arranged in artful clusters.

Decking the halls for Independence Day entertaining might also involve combining the national colors with other more personal patriotic touches in the way of heirloom family portraits and/or historical mementoes.

From big cities to small-town America alike, outfitting homes, buildings, streets, and landscapes for the Fourth was undertaken in no small way. *The New York Times* wrote evocatively in 1896 about the early morning hours when the city donned its "patriotic finery"—"*The forest of house-top poles flung their bunting to the breeze, and from windows and along house fronts everywhere loyal colors were soon displayed*"—and just as enthusiastically, almost two decades later, about the plans for updated nighttime illuminations.

> The lighting of parks, play-grounds, and other civic centres is to be on a larger scale this year than ever before attempted. The [Illumination] Committee already has arranged for the illumination of more than 100 civic centres and hopes to be able to enlarge this program. . . . Every citizen is asked to do something to add to the brightness of New York City, even if it be no more than to hang a Japanese lantern containing an electric light bulb out of his front window. The committee [also] recommends an American flag flooded with projected light.

The 1903 issue of *The Housekeeper*, on the other hand, captured the red, white, and blue enthusiasm typical of the nation's smaller cities and towns:

> The house facing the lawn is decorated in the national colors, the sort of bunting being used draped from one window to another in long loops, and dropping beneath the latter in fan effects held up at either side by groups of flags. The main entrance is likewise trimmed in streamers of red, white and blue, caught back to resemble portieres, with boughs of green and strands of flowers; above a great shield edged with tiny flags is suspended, and this ornament—made easily of bunting-covered cardboard—is flanked by spread eagles.

Vintage magazine photograph of decorated homes on Deerfield Street in Hartford, Connecticut (from "A Sensible Fourth of July," The Ladies' World, July 1908).

Since so many July 4 events were held outside, Mother Nature proved the ideal choice to cohost the festivities. "With its hot sunshine and deep shade, all nature beckons us to out-of-doors," wrote *Entertainments For All Seasons*, "and the labor of preparing to give an entertainment *indoors* is [actually] double one which is planned with Nature's vantage ground as the banquet hall, her own beauties as decorations, while the birds sing to the blue sky above, and the leaves of the trees stir in answer to the breeze."

Amongst the suggested fresh air venues were "pretty lawns," which were made all the lovelier with red, white, and blue paper lanterns hanging from the trees; "aromatic pine groves" where tree trunks were wound with the "tricolor of patriotism," their branches "fluttered" with star-tipped streamers; or even "vine-covered verandas" replete of "great, cool flagstones" and ample cushioned seating.

With carefully tended gardens at their disposal, Fourth of July hostesses typically imbued settings with abundant fresh flowers. *The Designer* (1903) recommended that tabletops be adorned with simple bouquets of red and white carnations displayed in tandem with blue "ragged sailors" as cornflowers or bachelor's buttons were commonly called.

Floral arrangements of columbine (either wild or cultivated), roses, geraniums, sweet alyssum, larkspurs, forget-me-nots, ageratums, and even violets were deemed suitable candidates for patriotic decorating duty. If real blossoms weren't available, handsome paper facsimiles could be made with the help of instructional guides like 1899's *Art & Decoration in Crepe & Tissue Paper*, published by the Dennison Manufacturing Company of Framingham, Massachusetts.

Hung by the dozens—if not the hundreds—at outdoor sites on the Fourth, lightweight paper Japanese- or Chinese-style lanterns were inexpensive choices for framing the scene with touches of whimsy and exotic flair. A reader of *The Ladies' World* recalled how the ephemeral novelties were used to decorate her neighborhood on the night of Independence Day 1912:

> The Japanese lanterns were strung on wires, a little sand having first been put in [their] bottoms to keep the wind from swaying them to and fro, from the posts of the porches to the branches of the trees along the curbstone. The lanterns were also used to illuminate the porch, being fastened to the roof at short distances of about six inches apart. . . . At dark all the lanterns were lit, making the street a myriad of fantastic colors.

Vintage embossed postcard marked "Fourth of July series No. 3." Postally unused.

Vintage real-photo postcard showing patriotically decorated neighborhood ca. 1915; marked "Rexo." Postally unused.

Vintage postcard marked "Copyright 1906 Osborne Ltd. NY 1353." Mailed Dallas, South Dakota, (day illegible) 1908.

Inside or out, the charmingly simple ways in which folks in the early twentieth century celebrated the "New and More Glorious Fourth" made the good 'ol summertime the perfect choice for entertaining in the old-fashioned way.

DECK THE PATRIOTIC HALLS

* *Come Rally Round the Flag.* "Decorate the porch and grounds with streamers of colored paper, flags and hanging baskets, the last named to be filled with red, white and blue flowers. These are easily made of cardboard boxes covered with crepe paper, and either paper or natural flowers can be used for them according to convenience." (*The Designer*, July 1913)

* *Uncle Sam's World.* "The table was beautifully adorned with red-and-white flowers and blue ribbons. In the centre of a wreath of smilax studded with tiny flags, astride of a small-sized school globe, perched a doll arrayed as Uncle Sam." (*The Designer*, July 1904)

* *A Red, White, and Blue Luncheon.* "The entire color scheme of this novel luncheon must be evolved in the national tints; as far as possible the doilies used should be designed in star-shaped patterns, with a border in wash silks of interwoven red carnations and blue corn-flowers. Suspended directly over the center of the table a huge liberty bell should be hung, composed of red and white carnations and blue corn-flowers. Descending therefrom should be ropes of red, white and blue ribbon, terminating at the four corners of the table. Draperies and pictures indicative of the occasion should be placed in conspicuous points of vantage." (*The Ladies' World*, July 1901)

* *Attractive Souvenirs of the Day.* "To make [the firecrackers] cut strips of uncooked macaroni into two or three inch lengths and run a piece of string through [their] centres, with ends protruding like a fuse. Next cover the macaroni with red paper. A little pile of them can be arranged in

front of each plate, or they can be piled in the centre of the table to give a most dangerous look to the table." (*The New York Times*, June 28, 1914)

* *Out on the Porch.* "Red, white and blue bunting was draped gracefully along the porch railing, Japanese lanterns hung at regular intervals, and tiny flags, stuck here and there through the vines that grew almost entirely around the porch, gave an air of festivity to the scene." (*McCall's Magazine*, July 1909)

* *Patriots from the Past.* "If you chance to be the happy possessor of the portrait of some revolutionary ancestor, let this form the centre of your decorations. Bring forward any relics of colonial times and make them hold a prominent place. Strips of bunting, cheese-cloth, or tissue-paper in red and white and blue are necessary, and must do their part in adding to the gayety of the scene. These can be arranged in festoons, and made into wreaths, stars, etc., to be used as ornaments on the walls." (*The American Girls Handy Book*, 1890)

* *An Independence Day Centerpiece.* "A drum, the drumsticks tied to the rim with patriotic ribbon and white carnations, makes an effective centerpiece, using miniature drums to hold the bonbons, and shields for place cards to decorate the candle shades." (*The Party Book*, 1912)

* *A Fourth of July Porch Party.* "The guests found the porch gaily and elaborately decorated with the Stars and Stripes, brilliantly illuminated by means of numerous small red, white and blue lanterns, and comfortably furnished with easy chairs. Suspended from the central arch of the porch was a liberty bell, composed of a framework of wire overlaid with smilax and red, white and blue asters. The beauty of this floral piece vies description, and elicited much praise." (*Entertainments For All Seasons*, 1904)

Vintage photograph. Ladies' Independence Day gathering ca. 1900.

Flags and other party goods (Dennison's Party Book, 1915).

Party table set with drum motifs and balloons (from "The Table on the Fourth of July," The Ladies' Home Journal, July 1904).

* *A Patriotic Table Setting.* "The centerpiece is made of four small American flags . . . with a small cardboard drum tied to the middle of each flag. The table is lighted by four electric candlesticks with white crepe-paper shades, decorated with American flags. A small American shield is placed on top of each folded napkin. Red, white and blue balloons might be floated over the table." (*The Designer,* July 1916)

* *A Luncheon for the Fourth of July.* "Each of the six tables was set for four guests. They were covered with blue cloths, over which white net covers were spread. The necessary touch of red was provided for in the centerpieces, which were bunches of scarlet geraniums arranged in tall glass vases, with dropping ferns to relieve their stiffness." (*The Modern Priscilla,* July 1904)

* *A Patriotic Sunset Tea.* "Small tables for the serving of the tea should be placed here and there, preferable under the shade of some tree. These should be covered with white cloths—a large bunch of flaming salvia placed in the center of each, either in blue bowls to give the necessary complement of color, or tied with a bow of blue ribbon. From the trees, red, white and blue Japanese lanterns should hang, to give their lights when the sun dies behind the hills." (*Entertainments For All Seasons,* 1904)

* *For Independence Day.* "The room . . . should be well decorated with flags and bunting of the national colors, while pictures of Revolutionary [themes] such as George and Martha Washington, the battle of Bunker Hill, the Boston tea party, Washington crossing the Delaware, the signing of the Declaration of Independence, the surrender of Cornwallis, etc., should adorn the walls. The table should be draped about the edge with tri-colored bunting and a knot of this or a flag draped about each chair. Secure a well-mounted American eagle to place in the center of the table, with a flag draped about the base." (*The Good Housekeeping Hostess,* 1904)

* *Novelties for a Fourth of July Party.* "Four small flags, tied

with a many-looped rosette of scarlet ribbon, may stand beside each plate with a place card attached to one of the ribbon ends. The napkins, of paper with flag decorations, should be hidden in four-inch sections of mailing tube, covered with scarlet paper and decorated with red-white-and-blue fringes and appliqué designs cut from paper doilies." (*The Delineator*, July 1907)

* *The Spirit of the Fourth*. "Decorate the dome of the chandelier with flags and a large outspreading 'patriotic flag' in the center. A pasteboard cannon-cracker, filled with candy, may be laid on each napkin as a souvenir." (*The Delineator*, July 1917).

* *A Patriotic Lawn Party*. "If the affair is an after-dark one, the lawn will have to be illuminated, which is best done, where electric lights are not convenient, with Japanese lanterns . . . the lanterns are caught on stout wires and swung between the house and trees, or if there be not a sufficient number of trees, are fastened to impromptu poles driven in the ground; the wires are garlanded in green, and at intervals bunches of flags float over the lanterns. Lawn benches, chairs and seats have their share of patriotic colors, and, being scattered here, there, and everywhere, lend to the general cheeriness of the attractive scene so thoroughly American." (*The Housekeeper*, July 1903)

* *POP! Goes the Chandelier*. "Very different in character is the firecracker centerpiece. Bunches of crackers are suspended from the chandelier at various heights with red, white and blue ribbon." (*The Party Book*, 1912)

* *A Girl's Fourth of July*. "A large United States shield can be made of colored paper or inexpensive cloth tacked on a piece of card-board, cut in the desired shape, and the shield suspended from the window flat against the house, as a picture is hung on the wall. Other emblems can be manufactured in the same way. Small trees or bushes covered all over from top to bottom with flags and streamers look beautiful, and all the gayer, when the wind blows, causing them to wave and flutter. Fasten the flags

Vintage real-photo postcard of a ca. 1910 home in patriotic regalia, marked "KOKO." Postally unused.

Crepe paper decorations for chandeliers and light fixtures (*Dennison's Patriotic Decorations and Suggestions, 1918*).

Vintage postcard marked "ZIM." Postally unused.

and streamers on the tree with string." (*The American Girls Handy Book*, 1890)

* *A Fourth-of-July Party for Children.* "Around the lawn into the grape arbor . . . the supper table has been set. There are tiny flags stuck into the vines all around, and from the center of the roof streamers of red, white and blue crepe-paper come down to the table, forming a canopy. In the center of the table is a beautiful red, white and blue bouquet made of red and white roses and blue bachelor buttons." (*McCall's Magazine*, July 1913)

* *A Fourth of July Dinner.* "A miniature Uncle Sam, placed in the midst of the usual fern and vine dish, makes a charming and decorative centerpiece. Surround this dish with flags—if possible using forty-eight, one for each state. Hang from the chandelier a big Liberty Bell, with two cross flags above it. Use candles with red, white and blue [accents]." (*Good Housekeeping Magazine*, July 1914)

* *Feting the Fourth.* "At each table five places were set, with dainty crepe paper doilies of patriotic design, while the charming centerpieces, which gave a pretty touch of color, consisted of low bowls hidden by folds of red and white crepe paper and filled with deep blue pansies. These flowers, by the way, were tied with narrow red and white ribbon and presented to the guests." (*McCall's Magazine*, July 1909)

* *The Light of Freedom.* "In-door illumination . . . can be made very brilliant by simply using a number of lighted candles. More elaborate touches could be had by employing the use of heavy paper letter to spell the evocative words 'Liberty' and 'Independence' and gumming them to windows where they could be seen outside when they were lighted." (*The American Girls Handy Book*, 1890)

* *Miss Columbia's Tea Party.* "The table in the center, which has a crepe paper flag tablecloth and centerpiece of flags, is used as a serving table only. The window-shades are pulled down and the candles lighted, which give a very pretty effect and shows off the red, white and blue decorations

to good advantage. Red, white and blue bunting is draped all about the room." (*Entertainments For All Seasons*, 1904)

* *A Patriotic Meeting Place.* "The dining-room may be turned into a tent, with alternate strips of red, white and blue cheesecloth, meeting at the chandelier, carried and tacked to the picture moulding, and hanging thence to the floor. Tissue-paper shades of the national colors may envelop the glass ones of the lights and a liberty bell hung above the table. Any relics of Colonial times should be given prominence." (*The Ladies' Home Journal*, July 1904)

* *A Firecrackerless Fourth for Children.* "The dinner is eaten outdoors at a table made of long boards resting on horses and tastefully draped with bunting in the three colors, red, white and blue. Paper napkins in patriotic designs are folded in tent shape from the peak of which floats a tiny flag." (*New Idea Woman's Magazine*, July 1907)

* *Floral Fireworks.* "For the centre of the table have a firecracker plant, the blossoms of which are about an inch long, and in shape and color resemble a firecracker. Cover the pot with bright red tissue paper, and with large firecrackers form a five-pointed star on the table around the plant. Now, make a fringe of medium-sized firecrackers, by tying them at intervals of three or four inches, to bright red taffeta binding ribbon. Have two pieces of the ribbon, and make the fringe in the centre of each piece, and long enough to reach from the chandelier to the corners of the table, where the rest of the ribbon is fastened in large rosettes." (*The Household*, July 1901)

Dainty Accessories for Patriotic Tables

ALL of these favors are easy to copy from the pictures. No. 1. Serving Cup. Covered with red, white and blue rose petals. Seals P 430 used on the handle.

No. 2. A snapping bon bon made into a "lady" by the addition of wire arms and a full ruffled skirt. A face painted with water color and black crepe paper hair make her complete.

No. 3. Slashed crepe paper put around the foundation makes a "lantern" serving cup. Two Flags P 274 are tied to the handle.

No. 4. A serving cup is covered with buff and blue which forms a tricornered hat. The design cut from Place Card P 8 decorates it.

No. 5. Shield P 270 attached to piece of crepe covered wire which is bent in spiral shape is an attractive place card favor.

No. 6. A similar place card favor uses P 361 Hatchet. The cherries are made of crepe paper.

No. 7. Crepe paper wrapped wire and mat stock form the foundation of the "firecracker" which of course is red. The skirt is of tricolor ruffles.

The table decoration has for its motif Decorated Crepe P 558. The picture will be very easy to use as a model

Page eight

Decorated table surrounded by crepe and die-cut party favors (Dennison's Gala Book, 1923).

The Importance of the Decorations

Excerpted from *The Delineator*, July 1894

The patriotic American mother is anxious to celebrate Independence Day in such a manner as will impress her children with a sense of the freedom and independence which are their birthright. It devolves upon her to stimulate and encourage the patriotism of the younger members of the family by bringing to their minds as impressively yet as gayly as possible the significance of the anniversary, and this she can do by an artistic decoration of the home with the national colors, and by a menu and table ornamentation that will be viewed with delight and remembered ever after with joy.

Boys are especially well pleased to enter with enthusiasm and happiness into the spirit of the occasion, and if they do not collect flowers that can be used in a decorative manner, such as sweet peas or the numerous wild flowers that can be found in red, white and blue, they can at least assist in draping the dining-room with the national colors. The large flag of silk or bunting will be in demand, and its possibilities for artistic draping will be made the most of.

The center-piece for the table could be a fortress made of fire-crackers surmounted by a small silk flag; or the red, white and blue could be grouped in a floral piece that would not at this season be too expensive. At each plate should be laid a small bunch of flowers tied with red, white and blue ribbons, and bonbons in red, white and blue papers should be conspicuously displayed in a fanciful dish, while a very small and dainty bow or rosette of the colors should be worn by each of the diners.

DO ME A FAVOR

Party Novelties with Panache

"Grown folks, as well as children, like to 'make-believe,' and are always best pleased with the party at which the dishes, favors and decorations are symbolic of that particular day."

McCall's Magazine, July 1912

In the early 1900s, hostesses of every stripe (or star!) depended on favors and clever souvenirs to double their guests' pleasures at holiday get-togethers; when it came to safe and sane parties on the Fourth, however, novelties and trinkets also served to provide guests with some fireworks-free amusements to enjoy.

Party crackers (also known as "mottoes," "snapping bon-bons," or simply "crackers") were decorated crepe-paper-covered tubes each of which contained a folded tissue paper hat, an inexpensive trinket, and a piece of paper bearing a joke or conundrum. The booty within was revealed with a *POP!* when both of the cracker's fringed ends were pulled simultaneously. The extremely popular novelties doubled as decorations for the dinner table or, as suggested by *McCall's Magazine* in 1915, could be used to "give the party a jolly ending."

Place settings were also enhanced with individual candy containers that resembled small firecrackers, tiny drums, or diminutive "cocked" hats; beautifully lettered souvenir menu cards; or patriotic place cards. Choices of a more interactive variety included hand-held paper fans (certain to be appreciated by guests seeking blessed relief from the heat) and noisemakers (the better for youngsters to create the ubiquitous racket of the day). Especially popular amongst noisemakers were the sturdy novelty horns made by decorating recycled cardboard yarn cones and fitting them with whistle mouthpieces.

Easily *the* most popular novelty at early-twentieth-century parties, though, were the intriguing decorative repositories of party favors known as Jack Horner "pies."

The Glorious Fourth

The Fourth of July would be indeed a dull day without sports, games, gay parades and parties.

"Johnnie Firecracker" himself furnishes the theme for the table decoration shown. Red mat stock, crepe paper and wire are the materials from which he is made.

Smaller "Johnnies" are performing all kinds of funny antics perched on the nut cups, and lollypops with firecracker hats make favors which also serve as place cards. Around the table Decorated Crepe Paper P 25 is used, the field with its stars at the top and the red strips cut in pennant shape flying below it.

We must all be children in spirit on this day, so favors for the children can be used for the grown-ups as well. Small fans of cardboard made in star shape and covered with red, white and blue crepe paper will be acceptable for the girls, and the boys, big and little, can have fun with tricolor pin wheels attached to clothes pins.

Another way to use a lollypop is in the shape of a firecracker candy box. It is very simple to make as is also the star serving cup. The serving cup form is covered with ruffles of red, white and blue. A star made of mat stock covered with silver paper which has the center cut out is slipped up and fastened in place just below the flaring ruffles.

Firecracker-topped table setting and assorted party favors (Dennison's Gala Book, 1922).

In its simplest form, the Jack Horner pie was a large pan or other container decorated to suit the occasion and filled with tiny gift-wrapped novelties that were designed to be pulled from within when guests tugged at leads of color-coordinated ribbon.

The Party Book (1912) offered the following account of the merry tradition:

> Ever since the days when hungry Jack Horner was first put on record as having "put in his thumb and pulled out a plum," the favor pie, in one guise or another, has been a popular feature of parties for grown-up children as well as for their juniors. In the beginning, the lines of little Jack's own famous pastry were followed as closely as possible, the "pie" usually consisting of a receptacle ranging from a milk-pan to a wash-tub, filled with bran in which tissue-wrapped trinkets were concealed, and covered with a more or less realistic paper "crust."
>
> By degrees, however, the original form was superseded by more fanciful shapes, so that the name became a decided misnomer; yet all attempts to evolve a new title having lamentably failed, any device in which small favors are concealed is still in popular parlance a "Jack Horner Pie," though its outward semblance may be that of a rose, a cabbage, or even a plum pudding!

"For children parties, there is nothing which gives so much pleasure than the Jack Horner Pie," mused *The Doll's Dressmaker Magazine* in 1892. "[We] have seen older people find quite as much amusement in them, and in these days when at every luncheon and dinner party there are favors furnished for each guest, this makes a novel and amusing way to distribute them."

In honor of the Fourth, "Jack Horners" were popularly disguised as oversized firecrackers, patriotic shields, Liberty Bells, and even faux "cakes." For the most part, these combination centerpiece/treasure chests were relatively simple to put together, even for the craft-impaired—after all, no matter how lavish (or humble) the "pie," it was meant to be torn apart for guests to retrieve the prizes hidden inside!

PLACE CARDS

* "Pretty and suitable place cards may be made by simply using [a] flag seal on a large plain white card, on which is

written in blue or red ink a patriotic or famous saying by a noted American, such as the following:

'I only regret that I have but one life to give my country' . . . Nathan Hale

'I am an American—and wherever I look up and see the Stars and Stripes overhead, that is home to me.' . . . Oliver Wendell Holmes." (*The Book of Games and Parties for All Occasions*, 1920)

* "Appropriate place cards for a Fourth of July luncheon or dinner may be made by covering small glass bottles about the size of a medium large fire cracker with red tissue paper and filling them with little candies. By cutting the corks even with the bottles and drawing a small piece of twine through for a fuse, a clever imitation of a fire cracker may be made. The names of the guests may be written vertically on the bottles." (*Red Letter Day Parties*, ca. 1920)

* "Paper dolls make delightful place-cards for a patriotic luncheon. These little maidens are dressed in white paper dresses with red or blue sashes and hats of the same tint, or robed in dark blue paper with wee stars pasted on, a red sash and white hat with a red paper plume. Miss Liberty will be most suggestive of the flag of her country." (*The Designer*, July 1911)

* "Tiny flags may be placed at each plate to be used as boutonnieres. The name-cards may have patriotic quotations written on one side; the following are suitable:

Day of Glory! Welcome Day!
Freedom's banners greet thy ray.
To mark this day we gather round
And to our nation's founders raise
The voice of gratitude and praise.
Thou art the shelter of the free,
The home, the port of Liberty."
(*Entertainments For All Seasons*, 1904)

* "One clever hostess took small sheets of writing paper . . . using red or blue ink. These sheets were rolled, tied with blue

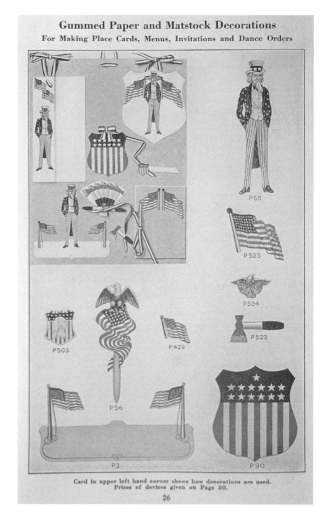

Patriotic stickers and decorative die-cuts for adorning place cards, menus, invitations, and dance cards (Dennison's Party Book, 1918).

Cardboard Uncle Sam cut-out No. P-366 (4" high) and double-sided cardboard Uncle Sam cut-out No. P59 (3¾"). The latter was used to decorate dishes of flavored ices; both are ca. 1910s-20s from Dennison Mfg. Co.

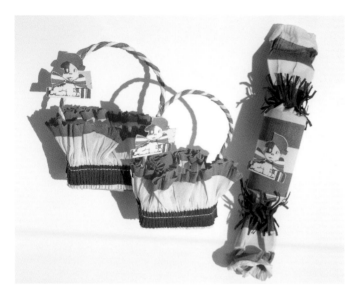

Vintage patriotic crepe paper nut cups and party crackers.

ribbon, sealed with red, and the guest's name written on the outside, the words 'Constitution of the United States' placed under each name." (*The Housekeeper*, July 1908)

CANDY CONTAINERS AND FAVORS

* "Place a little silk flag beside each plate. Every guest can pin this souvenir on dress or coat at the end of dinner." (*McCall's Magazine*, July 1908)

* "The napkins, of paper with flag decorations, should be hidden in four-inch sections of mailing tube, covered with scarlet paper and decorated with red-white-and-blue fringes and appliqué designs cut from paper doilies. In addition to the napkin, each of these holders may contain a favor, such as a Liberty cap, if for a lady, or a patriotic rosette—to be attached to the coat lapel—for a gentleman. To the base of each rosette or cap fasten a short piece of narrow ribbon by means of which it may be drawn through the tube without danger of tearing on removal." (*The Delineator*, July 1907)

* "Have a flagstaff made of a broomstick covered with paper, rising from a bed of red and white carnations and blue larkspur. Tiny candies and fortunes can be rolled up in the flag, which is ready to raise when the guests sit down. When it is pulled to the top of the pole with baby ribbon the sweets are scattered over the table to the delight of the young people." (*The Designer*, July 1913)

* "Cut little squares of tissue-paper to make 'torpedoes' filled with small red candies. Scattered over the grounds in hiding-places, they will give the children something to hunt for after supper." (*New Idea Woman's Magazine*, July 1907)

* *"As each guest enters he or she should be presented with a tiny flag tied with tri-color ribbon which is intended to be pinned in some conspicuous position on the coat or [shirt]. Snap crackers containing tri-color Liberty caps may also be given out." (The Designer, July 1901)*

* "Imitation giant firecrackers for souvenirs may be made of plain manila wrapping paper folded compactly round and round with a heavy piece of cord in the center to represent a fuse. Plain red tissue paper is used for covering the firecracker. Ordinary talcum powder boxes covered with the red paper, and with a cord thrust through a wound paper fuse, as described in the foregoing, may be filled with bonbons." (*Entertainments For All Seasons*, 1904)

* "Little 'torpedoes,' small pieces of white tissue paper twisted about bonbons, may be passed frequently. Around each bonbon is found a wee strip of paper on which is written a conundrum. The answering of these will be pleasant fun for all when supper is in progress." (*The Housekeeper*, July 1908)

* "The favors at the table consisted of huge imitation firecrackers. These were made by covering empty [round] boxes with red paper. The top also was covered and a little hole made in [it] to admit the entrance of the end of a bit of wick from a candle which was securely glued under the paper. The covers of these boxes came off and inside were to found torpedoes—delicious little bonbons covered with tissue paper which was given the desired twist at one end." (*The Modern Priscilla*, July 1904)

* "A medium sized platter is passed to each guest with a folded patriotic napkin on it, on which rests a horn wrapped in striped paper. When the horn is emptied of the bonbons concealed therein, it is found to be bona fide, as is proved by the tootings." (*Entertainments For All Seasons*, 1904)

* "When the children open their packages [they find] a small American flag, a 'musical instrument,' and a head dress—'Uncle Sam' hats for the boys, flower caps for the girls." (*Entertainments For All Seasons*, 1904)

* "Cut 5"x7" lengths of red and white tissue-paper and fringe the seven-inch edges. Lay a white paper inside a red, wrap a joke into a paper ball, and roll the center of the two tissue-papers, tying on each side with narrow ribbon. It will look like the real paper motto." (*The Designer*, July 1913)

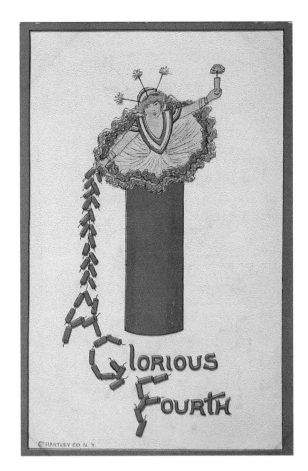

Vintage postcard marked "Hartley Co." Postally unused.

Party favors (Dennison's Gala Book, 1926).

Vintage red, white, and blue cardboard party hat with expandable white tissue honeycomb top.

DENNISON'S PARTY BOOK

Napkins, Place Cards and Serving Cups in Red, White and Blue

In the group of Patriotic Table Decorations illustrated at the left will be found American Eagle Napkin, No. P1025, made of extra heavy crepe paper.

Nut cup made by covering a plain cup with three little fan-shaped ruffles of crepe paper, one each red, white and blue, with Flags No. P54 and Seals P430 added. Paper Plate No. 601.

At the right the illustration shows two table articles that may be used on patriotic occasions.

Paper Plate No. 801 with handle made of wire and decorated with Uncle Sam Cut-outs No. P67. A ruffle of red crepe paper No. 81 finishes the effect.

Plain Cup with wire handles attached, then covered with a ruffle of crepe paper. Shield decoration cut from Napkin No. P500.

Paper napkins and decorative serving containers (Dennison's Party Book, 1921).

MENU CARDS

* "The menu card should have at the top a flag, either a real one fastened on or one put with colors. At the bottom a drawing of the cracked Liberty bell would be in keeping, while at either side attach a genuine firecracker." (*The Good Housekeeping Hostess*, 1904)

* "For favors, have flag fans, which can be bought for a trifle; on the back of the fans write the menu." (*The Household*, July 1901)

* "In case menu cards are desired, very thin note paper of narrow size should be selected. After writing the menu, it is rolled up, surrounded by a thin red paper, and lightly pasted shut. A bit of twine, secured to the centre by a drop of mucilage, forms a fuse for the 'firecrackers.'" (*The Designer*, July 1902)

JACK HORNER "PIES"

* "A Jack Horner pie in the form of a drum is a good centrepiece. The gifts, of course, are attached to the ends of ribbons which are thrust through the head of the drum. This drum can be made out of a hat box, covered with red, white and blue paper." (*The New York Times*, June 28, 1914)

* "The centerpiece consisted of a large bell suspended slightly above the table. This in reality was a large box, and opened in four sections when the ribbon which was attached to the tongue was pulled. Inside were concealed wee red drums, laced with gilt cord, and filled with small candies. Attached to these novel favors were red ribbons, one leading to each plate." (*The Mother's Magazine*, July 1910)

* "The last treat is the 'Fourth of July Pie,' which stands by itself on the small corner table. Each child is given a red, white and blue ribbon, one end of which a miniature Miss Columbia holds in her hands. For the foundation of her pedestal, the pie, an ordinary deep baking dish can be used to hold the souvenirs, and this should have a full fluted ruffle of crepe paper over it and around the edges. When the hostess gives

the signal, they all pull their ribbons, and each finds a small papier mache animal with a red, white and blue ribbon tied around its neck." (*Entertainments For All Seasons,* 1904)

* "A 'Yankee Doodle' pie [can be] made with red, white and blue tissue-paper covering a pan. Feathers from Chanticleer's tail are stuck in all over the top, one for each guest. At a given signal all pull up their feather and attached to it is a varied assortment of Fourth of July souvenirs—chocolate firecrackers, flag pins, liberty bells, tiny pincushions, and the like." (*New Idea Woman's Magazine,* July 1907)

* *Shield Pie.* "Place a dish on this centerpiece which will hold the souvenirs characteristic of the day—tiny cannons, flags, and so forth, all wrapped in red, white and blue paper and tied with narrow ribbon showing the national colors, each piece of ribbon being attached to a silver star. Over the top of the dish place a shield, made of red, white and blue paper, concealing the dish with [crepe paper] blossoms. This 'pie' can have a place on a small table at one side . . . and at the close of the meal the guests can draw their prizes." (*The Housekeeper,* July 1908)

* *Cocked Hat Centerpiece Filled With Favors.* "The hat brim is a red circle 17 inches in diameter, the crown a band 5 inches wide and 28 inches long. Brim and crown are held together with tabs of gummed cloth tape. Patriotic crepe paper covers the crown and is gathered in at the center of the top. The favors are pulled through this crepe top." (Dennison's *Party Book,* 1918)

* *Natural Flowers as Jack Horners.* "A beautiful effect is produced by using a natural rosebush, the gifts being wrapped in green and consequently invisible amid the foliage. The hostess, toward the close of the evening, cuts off a rose for each guest, who then discovers the attached trinket. Where economy must be considered, paper roses can be tied to the branches of a small shrub. Cut flowers may also serve the purpose of a Jack Horner. When used as a table centerpiece, ribbons are tied to the stems, and the flowers drawn forth by guests at the end of the meal." (*The Party Book,* 1912)

* "The children gather round [the Jack Horner pie] and are

Vintage embossed postcard marked "Fourth of July Series No. 3." Postally unused.

7" horn-style noisemakers made from sturdy cardboard spools recycled from use in textile mills ca. 1910s-20s. Left to right: Dandy Horn with wooden mouthpiece, E-Z Blow horn with metal mouthpiece, Bugle Horn missing mouthpiece.

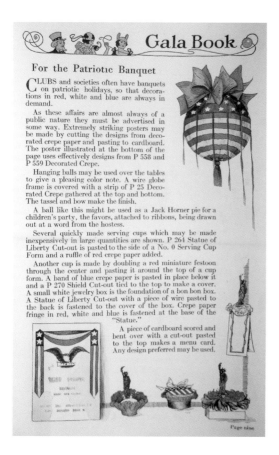

Gala Book

For the Patriotic Banquet

CLUBS and societies often have banquets on patriotic holidays, so that decorations in red, white and blue are always in demand.

As these affairs are almost always of a public nature they must be advertised in some way. Extremely striking posters may be made by cutting the designs from decorated crepe paper and pasting to cardboard. The poster illustrated at the bottom of the page uses effectively designs from P 558 and P 559 Decorated Crepe.

Hanging balls may be used over the tables to give a pleasing color note. A wire globe frame is covered with a strip of P 25 Decorated Crepe gathered at the top and bottom. The tassel and bow make the finish.

A ball like this might be used as a Jack Horner pie for a children's party, the favors, attached to ribbons, being drawn out at a word from the hostess.

Several quickly made serving cups which may be made inexpensively in large quantities are shown. P 264 Statue of Liberty Cut-out is pasted to the side of a No. 0 Serving Cup Form and a ruffle of red crepe paper added.

Another cup is made by doubling a red miniature festoon through the center and pasting it around the top of a cup form. A band of blue crepe paper is pasted in place below it and a P 270 Shield Cut-out is tied to the top to make a cover. A small white jewelry box is the foundation of a bon bon box. A Statue of Liberty Cut-out with a piece of wire pasted to the back is fastened to the cover of the box. Crepe paper fringe in red, white and blue is fastened at the base of the "Statue."

A piece of cardboard scored and bent over with a cut-out pasted to the top makes a menu card. Any design preferred may be used.

Page nine

Patriotic favors and large crepe paper hanging ball. The ball can serve decorative use only or it can be outfitted with ribbon leads and employed to distribute favors "Jack Horner"-style (Dennison's Gala Book, 1923).

Early twentieth-century novelty cigar fan. The cigar's tip can be pushed down and pulled back up again to disguise (or reveal) the flag-motif fan. Made in Japan.

told to select one of the red, white and blue ribbon rosettes which decorate [it]. At a signal all pull—thus demolishing the pie with its fluted crepe paper cover, securing a souvenir like toy cannons, candy crackers, various trifles." (*Entertainments For All Seasons*, 1904)

* "A large 'bomb' [firecracker] covered with red paper and filled with confetti may be suspended above the table and in it can be hidden little favors for each guest. Red ribbons attached to each favor hang out of the 'bomb,' one ribbon leading down to each plate. After luncheon the ribbons are pulled and the bomb 'explodes.'" (*Woman's Home Companion*, July 1915)

PARTING GIFTS

* "When supper is over, the hostess announces a hunt for firecrackers and torpedoes hidden in the grass and shrubbery. The firecrackers are of candy, wrapped in paper. The torpedoes are squares of red, white or blue paper in which . . . salted nuts or red and white bonbons are tied. Bunches of harmless sparklers are then passed and these are lighted just at twilight as the children start for home." (*Entertainments For All Seasons*, 1904)

* "Wee flower pots, some of white and some of blue, can each hold a small plant in bloom, either at the covers or as departing gifts as the guests wend their ways home under the 'stars in the blue.'" (*The Housekeeper*, July 1908)

* "Small fans of cardboard made in a star shape and covered with red, white and blue crepe paper will be acceptable for the girls, and the boys, big and little, can have fun with tricolor pin wheels attached to clothes pins." (Dennison's *Gala Book*, 1922)

* "Dainty souvenirs [given] by the hostess . . . may consist of a framed picture of Washington; a bound volume of 'The History of the Flag'; a box of bonbons tied with a rosette of red, white and blue ribbon; a padded and perfumed hanger covered with a small silken flag; [or] a fancy box of candy in the form of a large firecracker." (*The Designer*, July 1904)

FOOD FOR THE FOURTH

"The menu was a poem. Tiny clams on the half-shell on a bed of cracked ice, served with halves of limes and the crispiest of wafers; cream of asparagus soup; deviled crabs, dressed with cucumbers; broiled mushrooms on toast; spring lamb with mint sauce and green peas; boiled new potatoes with butter sauce; a salad of small, chilled whole tomatoes on crisp lettuce with mayonnaise; cream cheese and toasted crackers, followed by ices, strawberries and cream, cocoa and bonbons."
The Modern Priscilla, July 1902

Squabs on Toast? Truffled Partridge Sandwiches? Tongue in Aspic? *Really!?* Yes . . . really.

If entrées like these aren't exactly what comes to mind when you envision meal options for the Fourth of July, welcome to Independence Day dining circa 1900, a bygone era when about the only thing diners *could expect* was to see something *unexpected* on the party menu.

Formal dinners have been a Fourth of July tradition dating back to the celebratory meal at Philadelphia's City Tavern that marked the first anniversary of American independence. Never ones to skimp when it came to entertaining, hostesses of the decorous early twentieth century kept up the custom. *The Household* (1901) exemplified the era's formality when it counseled homemakers to "call into requisition for the table-service and adornment of the dining-room all the antique china, silver, candlesticks, candelabra, and the like, which she may be fortunate enough to possess." Yes indeed . . . great-grandmother's silver and china *for the Fourth of July!*

Menu wise, Independence Day hostesses occasionally served up some decidedly unappetizing party fare, even if the times are taken into account, like the aforementioned Tongue in Aspic ("*Thank Goodness!*" wrote reassuring

"Our Patriotic Party July 4" by artist Frances Tipton Hunter
(The Children's Party Book, 1924).

magazine editors at *The Delineator*, July 1894, "*this meal-time essential is now available in convenient cans!*"); Ham and Tongue *a la* Valley Force (*did anyone* really *think that either a continental name or a noble historical link would make this dish palatable?*); Creamed Tongue (*you don't want to know*); and Olive-and-Tongue Sandwiches ("*Delicious!*" exclaimed a food editor at *McCall's Magazine*).

Contemporary tastebuds shutter.

Fortunately for hungry partygoers, hostesses were also encouraged to prepare other more palatable, if not entirely casual, main dishes such as Creamed Lobster in Pastry Shells, Jellied Chicken (which, hopefully, still tastes like chicken), Leg of Lamb with Mint Sauce and Currant Jelly, and Fish Croquettes.

In addition, *McCall's Magazine* (1908) reminded their readers about the "old-established rule with some housekeepers to serve either lamb and peas, or boiled salmon and peas at the Fourth of July dinner," thus accounting for the plethora of recipes for both salmon (curried salmon, minced boiled salmon, salmon loaded with parsley cream sauce, lobster and salmon salad, salmon croquettes) and lamb (breaded lamb chops, crown of lamb with tiny new beets, broiled lamb chops in paper frills) that appeared in the July issues of popular magazines. Just don't forget to pass the peas!

Thankfully, all was not entirely lost in the Independence Day kitchens of yesteryear. Diners could also look forward to ample servings of fresh fruit (from chilled watermelon to currants, berries, and bananas) and vegetables (such as tomatoes, whether baked, stuffed, jellied, or served as salads) as well as an abundance of enticing desserts like pies, cakes, cookies, and the ever-popular bonbons. Frozen fruit ices and homemade ice creams made especially refreshing finales to the repast.

The Independence Day menus of yesteryear were meant to please the eyes as well as eager taste buds. *The Delineator* pulled out the full complement of red, white, and blue stops for its 1910 "American Flag Dinner."

> The red dishes may include a fruit salad of strawberries, red raspberries, currants and cherries, or they may be served *au naturel* for the fruit course. Follow with a red soup, such as tomato or lobster bisque, or a white one like cream of clams with whipped cream.

The relishes would be red radishes, little white onions or salted popcorn. The fish would be bluefish and the *piece de resistance* could be roast beef very rare or a white fricassee of chicken. Cold Westphalia or Virginia ham can also be utilized. The vegetables can be white potatoes mashed and beaten to creamy lightness, asparagus or cauliflower with cream sauce and cucumbers.

The salad may be of tomato and cream cheese, and the dessert steamed blueberry pudding, followed by strawberry and lemon ice.

A cake frosted with white and decorated with blue violets, glaced and red crystallized cherries will carry out the color-scheme still further, as also will the grape-juice punch, with red cherries and white grapes.

Hostesses of the early 1900s also believed that inventive, or "cunning" as it was popularly said in post-Victorian parlance, food presentations enhanced the dining experience, an approach that brought many a novel dish to the holiday table. Potatoes might be presented as cannon balls or "roses." (To make "roses," press hot, seasoned potatoes through a decorating tube onto a buttered tin, brush with egg yolk, delicately brown in a hot oven.) And virtually any foodstuff, from bite-size pieces of sponge cake to bonbons and deviled eggs, could be wrapped to look like torpedoes, the popular impact fireworks in top-tied tissue-paper packaging that resembled small sachets themselves.

Little souvenir American flags adorned cakes; cupcakes were iced to resemble tiny drums; and reusable novelty molds were used to create ice cream renditions of cannons, Uncle Sam, and the flag.

On a purely decorative note, *The Household* (1902) told its readers how to fashion decorative "radish roses":

Select medium-sized, round radishes for the roses. Beginning at the root end, make incisions at equal distances apart, cutting within a quarter of inch near stem end; then with a pointed knife—a pen knife—separate the red petal portions from the white, and you will have a semblance to the blossom carrying out the red and white color scheme.

Vintage postcard with embossed edges marked "Fourth of July Series No. 9." Postally unused.

National Cake

"National Cake" (from "A Fourth of July Luncheon," The Household, July 1902).

Vintage embossed postcard marked "'4th July' Series Number 705." Postmark illegible.

Vintage embossed postcard marked "PFB No. 8252." Double postmark on front of card: partial postmark of New Haven, no date, on bottom; full postmark of Hartford, Connecticut, July 3, 1908, on top.

Yet another way to serve food in the spirit of the day was to christen dishes with patriotic names. Columbia, the Gem of the Ocean was a fish salad; Star Spangled Banners were small star-shaped cakes decorated with flags; and Liberty Bells were bell-shaped sandwiches.

Picnics have long been associated with Fourth of July dining, and sandwiches, which are easy to make, convenient to transport, and likely to please myriad palates, were a top menu choice for hostesses with many hungry guests to feed.

"The *piece de resistance* of the picnic lunch is obviously the sandwich," *The Delineator* observed in 1894. "There was a time when the only known form of sandwich was made by simply placing a slice of meat between two slices of bread . . . but nowadays the advanced housekeeper scorns such a crude production and prepares instead sandwiches that are marvels of daintiness and goodness."

And what fanciful fillings they were! Gruyére cheese and mustard. Lobster on brown bread. Egg and watercress. Nasturtium and cucumber. Peanut and fig. Date and raisin.

Another Fourth of July picnic standard might have been popular for reasons other than taste. Deviled eggs were said to have been served once-upon-an-old-fashioned time by proper young ladies hoping to spark romantic interest from potential suitors.

Ultimately, the most important thing to pack for the outing was an ample sample of "true picnic spirit."

"All picnickers should expect to endure many little inconveniences without complaint," counseled *The Delineator* in 1894. "It is a small matter to see a harmless spider or a large ant promenading across the table-cloth, but the spirit of a true philosopher is needed if one is to bear with equanimity the discovery that the sandwiches taste hopelessly of the bananas, and the fried chicken of the cake."

So dive right in for a closer look at some other examples of Independence Day dining customs straight from the "good old days." Picky eaters needn't hold their RSVPs: no recipes for tongue, canned or otherwise, can be found herein.

FOOD PRESENTATION

(NOTE: *In the interest of authenticity, these vintage "receipts" have been presented in their original pinch-of-this, pinch-of-that narrative forms. Contemporary cooks are on call to add their own "pinches" of imagination to the mix.*)

* "Get lady-fingers made extra large and stack them like muskets, tying with red, white and blue ribbon, and have flags stuck in these. Make refreshing sandwiches of cream cheese with a little chopped olive and walnut-meats stirred in, and tie these, either rolled or flat, with patriotic baby ribbon. Lemonade can be colored pink with strawberry-juice, and served in blue cups. The little crackers known as cheese tidbits can be rolled in squares of colored tissue-paper to suggest torpedoes." (*The Designer,* July 1913)

* "Fill one blue dish with red and white currants; another with raspberries, white and red; a third with a ring-mould of tomato jelly enclosing the salad with white mayonnaise; a fourth with thirteen star-shaped cakes, iced in white. Chicken pot, cup custard, pandowdy and other old-fashioned dishes should form part of the menu. Pineapple or lemon and currant ices in blue dishes may be served later." (*The Ladies' Home Journal,* July 1904)

* "Have a porch table set forth with fans, and a bowl of lemonade or fruit punch. Beside the bowl, which can be wreathed with red, white and blue flowers, have a tray of tumblers and let the ladle have a gay knot of tricolored ribbon. If a blue punch-bowl can be obtained, red cherries floating in the lemonade will complete the color scheme." (*The Designer,* July 1913)

* "The viands may be in the national colors. Pressed salmon loaf and chicken loaf, sandwiches of currant jelly, or white lettuce and cream cheese blended with a little jelly to tint it; potato salad in red, white and blue cases. Also tomato jelly salad; red bananas and patriotic cakes—either slices of jelly roll or of cakes tied with blue and red ribbon. . . . The dessert may be a Charlotte russe with candied violets and cherries." (*The Housekeeper,* July 1908)

MINT JELLY BELLS

Left, "Mint jelly bells," a "toothsome" accompanied to crown of lamb; right, "Stuffed Cherries," fresh pitted cherries filled with a mixture of soft chocolate and chopped nuts (from "A Little Feast for the Fourth," The Designer, July 1906).

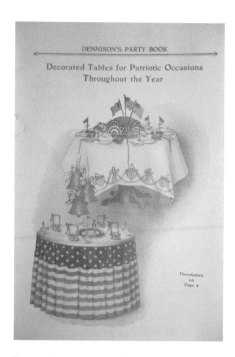

*Decorated patriotic tables (Dennison's
Party Book, 1921).*

*Wishing you
A Glorious 4th of July*

*Vintage embossed postcard marked "Fourth
of July Series No. 5." Postally unused.*

* "There are sandwiches of white bread with red peppers in the filling, tied with narrow blue ribbon; round red and white radishes in blue dishes; and the cutest individual tomato salads made of whole big scarlet tomatoes. There is a big cake frosted in white with red stripes across, and a toy cannon perched in the center. There are also some cunning tarts filled with red jelly, and little cup-cakes with blue frosting flowers." (*McCall's Magazine*, July 1913)

* "The ice cream or ices can be strawberry or red raspberry sprinkled with crushed violets, or when lemon ice or vanilla ice cream is used, cover with minced cherries and violets, or any of these may be molded in layers of red, white and blue, cutting in slices. The blue cream is made by using vegetable coloring." (*The Housekeeper*, July 1908)

* "There is a large mold of jellied red-tomato salad with star garnish of white potatoes, a plate of bell-shaped sandwiches, a plate of star cookies iced in the [patriotic] colors, iced tea; ice cream appropriately molded in bell forms will also be presented to the guests." (*The Book of Games and Parties For All Occasions*, 1920)

* "Platters of blue ware containing dainty minced chicken and tomato jelly sandwiches, small cut-glass and silver dishes holding white cream peppermints, red jelly gum-drops and salted nuts, with plates of small cake frosted with vanilla and strawberry icing, will give the table quite a festive air. A frozen dainty may also be served. . . . This may take the form of fresh strawberry cream, served in a blue Bohemian sherbet cup, and ornamented with a star of whipped cream, or small pasteboard boxes may be covered with red, white and blue crepe paper and filled with vanilla mousse." (*The Designer*, July 1904)

* "For the supper, have a firecracker salad, made from large red beets, well boiled and cut into the require shape with a small apple corer, and served on lettuce leaves. If using a mayonnaise dressing, do not allow it to be too much in evidence upon the beets, or the effect of the firecrackers will be lost." (*The Household*, July 1901)

* "First came plates of dainty salmon and lettuce sandwiches, with an accompaniment of small red radishes in little blue and white dishes. When justice had been done to these, the plates were removed and vanilla ice cream was served in old-fashioned blue and white dishes, with chopped candied cherries sprinkled thickly over each mound of cream. Small cakes, iced with white and decorated with halves of candied cherries, pressed on while the icing was still soft, were also served, and a tiny red, white and blue cornucopia, filled with salted nuts and plump raisins was laid beside each plate." (*McCall's Magazine*, July 1909)

* "We had consumed quantities of lemonade tinted a patriotic red and served in tall white glasses with blue crepe-paper frills. We had eaten cakes and cookies cut in appropriate shapes and covered with red, white, and blue icing. We had finished with ice cream similarly treated." (*McCall's Magazine*, July 1917)

* "Place imitation firecrackers on a large platter, surrounded by small cookies, in white tissue-paper, to represent torpedoes." (*The Designer*, July 1916)

* "The conventional dinner roll may be tied around with red, white and blue ribbon. When preparing the tomatoes, save the slice cut off the top, which is usually discarded. Bake it at the same time as the rest of the tomato. When done, the top will be dry, as it has little juice, and may have two slits cut into it, through which a tri-colored ribbon is passed and tied in a pretty bow. Place on the top of each tomato, as a lid." (*The Designer*, July 1902)

* "Various appetizing dishes can be prepared for a patriotic entertainment which will carry out the color scheme nicely. Lobster or tomato salad served on blue china with a white dressing, salted wafers tied with baby ribbon in red and blue, and ices and jellies tinted the desired shades, are all most effective." (*The Ladies' World*, July 1903)

"Independence Rolls," puff pastry rolls filled with a creamy seasoned egg mixture (from "A Little Feast for the Fourth," The Designer, July 1906).

Vintage postcard with embossed edges marked "Fourth of July Series No. 9." Postally unused.

Vintage embossed postcard marked "Fourth of July Series No. 8."
Postally unused.

* "Entrees, vegetables and salads may be served in little paper cases [that] afford much scope for the display of the tri-colors. These are easily made of thin cardboard formed into cylinders, with a bottom filled in. They are lined with waxed paper, and the ornamentation consists of three ruches of red, white and blue crepe paper made very full and fluffy and put on in overlapping rows." (*The Designer*, July 1904)

MENUS

A FOURTH OF JULY BREAKFAST
The Designer, July 1911

Cantaloupe or Red Raspberries
Molded Cream of Wheat
Radishes   Watercress
Brook Trout or Fried Chicken
Waffles   Coffee

A FOURTH OF JULY LUNCHEON FEAST
The Housekeeper, July 1908

Cold Sliced Lamb Loaf in Mint Bed
Radish and Cucumber Salad
Creamed Chicken Baked in Tomato Cups
Rolled Sandwiches   Olives   Celery
Liberty Cake   Chilled Watermelon
Iced Tea

MENU FOR A FOURTH OF JULY PORCH PARTY
Entertainments For All Seasons, 1904

Chicken Salad in Lettuce Cups
Olive Sandwiches   Cheese Straws
Orange Frappé   Lady Fingers
Fruit Punch

FOURTH OF JULY PICNIC MENU
The Delineator, July 1910

Cold Fried Chicken
Devilled Eggs   Baking-Powder Biscuits
Radishes   Home-made Pickles

Bunker Hill Sandwiches
Fourth of July Gingerbread   Nantucket Sprinkles
Lemonade

MENU FOR A PATRIOTIC CHILDREN'S PARTY
Entertainments For All Seasons, 1904

Lettuce Sandwiches   Chicken Salad
Cheese Straws   Salted Almonds
Patriotic Ice Cream
Angel Cake   Macaroons
Fruit Punch

MENU FOR DINNER ON THE FOURTH
The Household, July 1901

Bunker Hill Wedges [pineapple salad]
Bisque of Firecrackers [tomato soup]   Cannon Balls
Potatoes á *la* Torpedoes   American Victories [beets]
Friendly Aid [lemonade]
Nuts   Radishes   Olives
Liberty Bell Salad
Independence Pudding   Original States Cake
Coffee

MENU FOR A FOURTH OF JULY DINNER
The Book of Entertainments and Frolics For All Occasions, 1911

Clam Cocktails in Lemon Cups
Radishes   Salted Popcorn
Broiled Lobster
Cucumbers with French Dressing
Leg of Lamb with Mint Sauce and Currant Jelly
New Potatoes with Parsley
Tomato Salad   Cheese Straws
Watermelon or Cherry Pie
Coffee

AN IDEAL SUPPER
FOR FOURTH-OF-JULY EVENING
The Designer, July 1916

Cream of Chicken, with Broiled Mushrooms on Toast

Vintage embossed postcard marked "J-8." Postally unused.

Top, *jelly and farina molded patriotic dessert; bottom, cannon cracker-shaped gelatin and apple jelly dessert shaped using a scooped-out banana peel as a "mold" (from "Patriotic Dishes for the Fourth," McCall's Magazine, July 1912)*

Pair of red, white, and blue tables. The table at top was decorated using Patriotic Lunch Set No. P125, which consisted of one table cover and one dozen each of paper napkins, plates, and doilies. The set sold for sixty cents. Bonbon boxes and other matching pieces were sold separately (Dennison's Party Book, 1917).

Hot Biscuits
Iced Coffee with Whipped Cream
Tomato and Lettuce Salad with Mayonnaise Dressing
Cream-Cheese Balls on Red Rose-Leaves and Cornflowers
Rolled Peanut Sandwiches, tied with Red, White and Blue
Pineapple Souffle *a la* Firecracker
Torpedo Cookies

SUPPER FOR THE FOURTH OF JULY
The Ladies' World, July 1901

Salmon Croquettes   Washington Omelette
Tomato Salad
Virginia Biscuit   Peach Preserves
Seed Cake   Lemonade

RECIPES

~~~ BEVERAGES ~~~

* *Pour yourself an ice-cold glass of LEMONADE!*

• *Pink Lemonade.* "This is the way I made the punch: in the morning I boiled two cupfuls of sugar and two quarts of water for ten minutes; then I let it thoroughly cool, when I added the juice of eight lemons and one quart of strawberry juice. Each glass was partially filled with cracked ice and the beverage poured over it and a ripe strawberry floated on the top." (*McCall's Magazine,* July 1907)

• *Fancy Lemonade.* "Cut a neat slice from the top of as many lemons as are required, allowing one for each person. Scoop out the pulp, taking care not to break the skin, and with a lemon squeezer extract the juice. For each large lemon allow half a pint of water, and sweeten to taste with syrup made from granulated sugar and water cooked together until thick. Fill the lemon skins with the lemonade, replace the slice taken from the top after making a neat, round hole in it. Through the hole stick two straws with which to drink or suck up the liquid. Keep on ice what is left of the lemonade to replenish the lemon cups." (*McCall's Magazine,* July 1906)

• *Fourth of July Lemonade.* "The best lemonade is that

made with boiling water instead of cold. Three lemons make a quart of lemonade. Scrub and rinse the lemons. Chip off the thin outer skin of some of the lemons and steep for ten minutes in a little water. Press the juice from the lemon. Add to the juice sugar as desired, then pour on the proper amount of boiling water, together with the strained water from the chipped yellow peel. Let stand until cold, then if not ready to use, place in the ice-box until needed. Serve with slices of lemon, a couple to each glass. Slices of banana, strawberries cut in quarters, raspberries or pitted cherries add to the attractiveness of this beverage." (*The Delineator*, July 1910)

* *Fourth of July Punch.* "Make a very strong lemonade and add one bottle of claret; sweeten to taste. Cut slices of orange and pineapple and add, also strawberries and one cupful of currant juice. Put this in a punch bowl with a large block of ice." (*McCall's Magazine*, July 1909)

* *Liberty Frappé.* "To one pint of grape juice add a pint of water, the juice of a lemon, and sugar to taste. Freeze to a mush and serve in glasses with a spoonful of whipped cream and a candied cherry topping each one." (*The Ladies' Home Journal*, July 1914)

Vintage embossed postcard with shiny "gelatin" finish marked "1169." Postmark illegible.

~~~ STARTERS ~~~

* *Asparagus Fingers.* "Shred all of the edible part of the asparagus from the stalk. Mix thoroughly with a cream sauce, and spread on fingers of buttered toast ornamented with rounds of hard-boiled egg." (*The Modern Priscilla*, 1904)

* *(Oh You!) Deviled Eggs.*

  • *Recipe #1.* "Shell six hard-cooked eggs, cut lengthwise in half, remove yolks, mash them and add one teaspoonful *each* vinegar and melted butter, and ¼ teaspoonful *each* mustard, chopped parsley, and salt. Refill the whites and put pairs together. Wrap in tissue paper with frilled edges to represent torpedoes." (*A Thousand Ways to Please a Husband with Bettina's Best Recipes*, 1917)

Vintage embossed postcard. Postally unused.

"Tassel of Red, White and Blue," full ears of boiled sugar corn with tissue paper tassel ends (from "The Table on the Fourth of July," The Ladies' Home Journal, July 1904).

- *Recipe #2.* "Hard cook six eggs. Cut in half lengthwise. Remove the yolks. Mash the yolks and add salad dressing to make them of the consistency to shape. Add ¼ cup chopped pickle. Salt and pepper to taste. Make into oblong balls and fill the whites. Chopped ham or tongue [*is there no end to the canned tongue?*] may also be added." (*McCall's Magazine*, July 1920)
- *Recipe #3.* "Mash the yolks of hard-boiled eggs; add mustard, salt, pepper, enough vinegar to make the mixture moist, and a little chopped meat. When well mixed, mold into balls and return to the cavities in the whites of the eggs. A good variation of this is to add grated cheese instead of meat, and mayonnaise or cream salad dressing instead of vinegar." (*The Delineator*, July 1908)

* *Tomato and Lettuce Salad with Mayonnaise.* "Remove the top and center of the tomatoes, and stuff with green peppers and celery. Place on lettuce and serve with mayonnaise dressing." (*The Designer*, July 1916)

* *Fresh Cherry Salad.* "Stem and stone red cherries carefully to avoid losing their form. Insert a hazel-nut in the cavity left after removing the stones. Set on ice to chill. Or, line little blue cases with heart leaves of lettuce, mix the cherries with some white mayonnaise and place in the cases." (*The Designer*, July 1904)

* *Corn-and-Bean Salad in Tomato Cups.* "To one cupful of cooked sweet corn add one cupful of cooked white butter-beans, ½ cupful of chopped celery or a little chopped onion. Season well with salt and pepper and dress with a white boiled or mayonnaise dressing. Fill into tomato cups and chill." (*The Designer*, July 1917)

"Firecrackers and Torpedoes," paper-lined cardboard cases of frozen ice cream surrounded by peanut cookies wrapped in white tissue paper to resemble torpedoes (from "The Table on the Fourth of July," The Ladies' Home Journal, July 1904).

* *Cottage-Cheese with Various Additions.* "An appetizing mixture to serve with plain bread and butter or crackers is cottage-cheese, seasoned and also colored by having finely chopped pimento mixed through it. A novel arrangement is to mix only half of the cottage-cheese with the pimento, leaving the remainder white. Pack the two colors in even layers in an oblong mold, alternating the red with the white. When cold and firm, reverse on a blue plate, and slice off as desired." (*The Designer*, July 1915)

~~~MAIN DISHES~~~

* *Creamed Salmon á l'Americaine.* "Pick canned salmon into flakes, heat in cream sauce, and arrange in the center of hot mashed potatoes to resemble a fort. Top with a small American flag." (*The Designer*, July 1912)

* *Independence Day Crackers.* "To one can of salmon, drained and flaked, add six soda crackers, rolled fine, one tablespoonful of melted butter, three eggs, and sufficient sweet milk to make a mixture of the proper consistency to mold. Season to taste, shape like cannon crackers [oversized firecrackers], and fry in deep fat after rolling them in egg and cracker crumbs. Just before serving, insert a fuse of radish or celery in the upper end of each 'cracker,' and send to the table garnished with heart leaves of lettuce and quarters of lemon." (*The Party Book*, 1912)

* *Chicken with Mayonnaise.* "Use little china dishes or paper cases and break into them small pieces of lettuce for the bottom layer, and sprinkle lightly with oil, vinegar, pepper and salt. Add a slice of tomato, and on this place a little heap of chopped cold chicken. Cover the top with a good, thick mayonnaise sauce and in the middle place a large olive." (*McCall's Magazine*, July 1906)

* *Salmon in Potato Cups.* "Wash and boil large potatoes in their skins. When tender remove and set aside until cold, then remove skins and cut into halves. Form into cups by removing some of the potato. Dust the insides with salt and pepper. Take a can of red salmon and remove all skin and bones. Mix with this a thick tomato sauce, or white mayonnaise colored with a few drops of red fruit or vegetable coloring. Season with salt and paprika. Fill this mixture into the potato cups. Place each cup on an individual blue plate." (*The Designer*, July 1917)

Vintage embossed postcard marked "S129." Postally unused with salutation written on reverse.

Vintage embossed postcard. Postally unused.

~~~SANDWICHES~~~

* *Nasturtium Sandwiches.* "Nasturtium sandwiches are novel, and most people are very fond of them, especially when the flowers are gathered fresh from the garden. Drop them into ice water to crisp while the rest of the luncheon is being made ready. Cut the bread in thin slices and butter it. Place a thin layer of the yellow petals on one pungent leaf between the slices. No seasoning is required aside from a light sprinkling of salt, as the nasturtium has a delightfully distinctive flavor of its own." (*McCall's Magazine*, August 1910)

* *Fourth of July Sandwiches.* "Peel one large tart apple and grate it. Mix one cupful of cream cheese and two Tablespoonfuls of cream together, with salt and pepper to taste. Mix grated apple and cheese together and spread between thin slices of buttered brown bread." (*McCall's Magazine*, July 1910)

* *Chicken-and-Ham Sandwiches.* "Cream ⅓ cup of butter and mix with one cup minced chicken and one cup minced ham. Season with salt and a dash of cayenne. Spread on white bread." (*The Delineator*, July 1908)

* *Egg and Watercress Sandwiches.* "Cut some thin slices of bread and butter, and cover them evenly with fresh watercress, sprinkling with a little salt and some chopped chives or a very little grated onion. Now spread them thickly with hard-boiled yolks of eggs which have been rubbed through a sieve, place another piece of bread on the top and press together." (*McCall's Magazine*, August 1910)

* *Egg Cream Sandwiches.* "Mash the yolks of six hard-boiled eggs with a half-cupful of cottage or Neufchatel cheese; add four Tablespoonfuls of mayonnaise, a chopped sweet red pepper, and a ½ teaspoonful of salt. Mix well, and spread between thin slices of buttered bread." (*Good Housekeeping Magazine*, July 1914)

Vintage postcard marked "Copyrighted by the P Co." Postally unused.

* *Red-and-White Sandwiches.* "Combine two cupfuls of finely chopped boiled ham, one large chopped pimento, and one Tablespoonful good tomato catsup. Use as a filling between thin slides of white buttered bread. Roll up and tie with a blue ribbon." (*The Designer,* July 1917)

"Ready for a Salute," iced cake with patriotic decorations (from "The Table on the Fourth of July," The Ladies' Home Journal, July 1904).

~~~SWEETS~~~

* *Fruit Salad.* "For a tasty salad, scoop out the pulp of three large juicy oranges. Add to the pulp one cupful of grated pineapple, one cupful of cherries and two bananas cut into small pieces. Sweeten to taste, and add two or three tablespoonfuls of sherry or the liquor from a small bottle of Maraschino cherries, and stand the mixture on the ice to blend and chill. Serve with whipped cream." (*McCall's Magazine,* July 1908)

* *Salpicon of Fruits.* "White grapes, thoroughly chilled and halves, were heaped in the center of individual blue china fruit plates, then surrounded by a border of ripe currants. The whole was sprinkled with sugar." (*The Housekeeper,* July 1904)

* *Sweet Sandwiches.* "Mix chopped figs and dates very fine, moistening with a drop or two of lemon juice and use that as a filling. Chopped nuts can make part of the mixture. Spread on thin slices of white bread or cake." (*McCall's Magazine,* August 1910)

* *Freedom Cakes.* "Either cookies or rounds of pound-cake may serve as the foundation of this attractive holiday dish. Cover them smoothly with plain vanilla icing and decorate with stripes of blue radiating from a candied cherry in the center of each one." (*The Designer,* July 1912)

* *Sour Cherry Toast.* "Toast several slices of bread, then butter. Stew two cupfuls of stoned cherries without any water if possible, and sugar enough to sweeten well. When cold, pour over the toast, set on individual plates and on each put a spoonful of whipped cream. This can be made with slices of stale sponge cake if preferred." (*McCall's Magazine,* July 1906)

Vintage embossed postcard marked "P. Sander 440." Mailed Vallejo, California, July 6, 1911.

"Cherry Bombe," a frozen fruit and ice cream concoction (from "A Little Feast for the Fourth," The Designer, July 1906).

Vintage embossed postcard. Postally unused.

PICNIC TIPS FOR THE FOURTH OF JULY HOSTESS

* "The bread for making sandwiches [for the picnic lunch basket] should be 24 hours old, or it will not slice smoothly. Trim the crusts off if you wish an especially appetizing appearance, but don't forget to save the crusts to use for making bread-crums [sic] later. Cream the butter with a spoon before spreading the sandwiches, and don't put it on too thick. When the sandwiches are made, wrap them in paraffin-paper, or in a napkin wrung out of hot water." (*The Delineator*, July 1908)

* "For a large picnic it is best to have an individual box for each person. Line the boxes with waxed paper. Put fruit at the bottom of each, [several] sandwiches wrapped separately in waxed paper, a deviled or hard-boiled egg similarly wrapped, two slices of plain cake, and a tiny bag of salted almonds. On top put two paper napkins and a drinking-cup." (*Good Housekeeping Magazine*, July 1914)

* "A large hat should never be worn at a picnic. A close turban or sailor hat, with a parasol for shade, means a comfort, and a serenity of mind that the most picturesque large hat could never yield. A gauze veil is an excellent protection against sunburn." (*The Delineator*, July 1894)

* "As picnics are remarkable chiefly for the appetites they develop, there should be at least one substantial dish. Cold meats are the easiest to manage—boiled tongue [*oh, no! . . . not again*], fried or pressed chicken, beef or veal loaf. Meat and fish salad are relished." (*The Designer*, July 1913)

* "The filling for the sandwiches consisted of minced boiled salmon left over from the regulation Fourth of July dinner of salmon and green peas. Lettuce and radishes came from the hostess' own garden, and both cakes and ice cream were the work of her skilful [sic] hands." (*McCall's Magazine*, July 1909)

* "At each place may be [found] a firecracker box, which on being opened is found to contain bonbons, and on top a slip of paper requesting the guests to 'hunt for their supper.' A search about the grounds will finally reveal white baskets hanging from the tree boughs, hidden under bushes and other likely places. These are lined with blue or red paper and tied with red and white bows of crepe paper streamers. The merry couples will return to the table with an added appetite and with the spirit of fun encouraged to the jollity point." (*The Housekeeper*, July 1908)

Vintage embossed postcard marked "American Post Card 'Independence Day' Series No. 122, Subject No. 2321, Published by the Ullman Manufacturing Co." Mailed Somerville, New Jersey, July 4, 1911.

How to Carry Pie to a Picnic

The Ladies' World, July 1901

The Picnic Pie has been a topic for merry-makers for untold decades, and the Man Who Sat Down In It, a stock joke.

It is an elusive dainty for an out-of-door repast, as it is so difficult to transport without its juiciness permeating every part of the receptacle that carries the luncheon, yet as the finish for an *al fresco* meal it has a toothsomeness unequaled by any other delicacy of the table—that is, provided it is a fresh, luscious, jelly-like apple pie fresh from the oven.

Behold, a picnicker of many years' experience has solved the problem of a way to get it to the festive gathering safe and sound.

Place the pie upon another slightly larger plate beneath the one on which it has been baked, so that if it is juicy, nothing else will be touched by it. Over it invert a milk-pan. This will prevent anything from crushing the pie, and several layers of plate, pie and pan can be safely stowed at the bottom of a picnic basket, and the remainder of the eatables tightly packed in the remaining space.

DRESSING THE PATRIOTIC PART

"What could be more picturesque than a Liberty cotillion, with figures in national colors? Uncle Sam and Miss Columbia would surely be striking figures. The ladies in white gowns, and red, white and blue aprons, with shoulder knots of tri-color ribbon and small flags in their hair, and the men in spangled and striped ties, making a unique figure."
Entertainments For All Seasons, 1904

During the early years of the twentieth century, events of a festive nature often called for special attire and the Glorious Fourth was no exception. In order to infuse the day with a suitably patriotic atmosphere, Independence Day hostesses would often choose to present themselves in the guise of beloved national icons such as Columbia or Miss Liberty. That widely respected leader of trends and fashions, *The Ladies' Home Journal*, offered its own clever take on how to bring the past to life:

> For the Fourth of July luncheon arrange to have Betsy Ross herself seated in a small chair at center. A plot of lawn should be under her feet, from which are springing red, white and blue flowers. Over her lap place a small reproduction of the flag made by Betsy Ross, with the thirteen stars in a circle.

Dressing the part of Uncle Sam—always dapper in his red-and-white striped trousers, stovepipe hat, and star-spangled tails—was the hands-down choice for men and young boys alike. Since home sewing skills were plentiful in households at the turn-of-the-twentieth-century, pattern inspiration for Uncle Sam costumes as well as many more style choices for the ladies was routinely featured in popular fashion magazines like *The Delineator, McCall's, The Designer*, and others.

Women who possessed sewing skills could also

consider creating patriotic party garments from crepe paper. According to paper industry leader Dennison Manufacturing Company of Framingham, Massachusetts, this popular approach to costuming not only constituted part of the holiday fun in and of itself, but also was the perfect choice for "those who desire something entirely fitting, something original and absolutely fresh."

Paper costumes were made by either sewing or pasting "folds" (lengths) of crepe paper to plain muslin bases, or to old two-piece combinations consisting of "waists," as bodices were called, and petticoats, or slips, and then embellishing them with accents of ribbon, small die-cut decorations, streamers, and so on. Dennison advertised its crepe papers to be of the highest quality with a velvety texture that made them ideally suited to costume making. Products of particular interest to those interested in creating paper attire were the many patriotic patterns, replete with handsomely evocative designs that incorporated up to eleven colors each, and the "Imperial" line of solids. The latter boasted an expansive rainbow of colors. In the blue spectrum, for example, customers could choose between Celestial, Azure, National, Navy, or French.

The creative minds at Dennison also provided paper garment makers with the inspiration and how-to instructions they needed in the handy soft-covered holiday-themed books they published on a semiannual basis. Available from Dennison stores or by mail at a cost of five to ten cents apiece, these beautifully illustrated little volumes captured just how novel and affordable outfits could turn ladies into patriotic princesses, men into colonial gents, and youngsters into merry crepe-fringed incarnations of skyrockets.

Ever mindful of its mandate when it came to paper décor, Dennison booklets also provided guidance on outfitting cars and floats for Fourth of July parades. In later years, other paper companies like C. A. Reed of Williamsburg, Pennsylvania, and American Tissue Mills of Holyoke, Massachusetts, followed suit by offering their own promotional decorating how-to booklets.

In lieu of an actual costume, a hostess might decide to simply add various patriotic accents to something in her

"Columbia" crepe paper costume (Dennison's Party Book, *1918).*

Ca. 1905 red, white, and blue cardboard party hat with tricolor tissue honeycomb crown and standing tissue-topped firecracker decoration.

existing wardrobe. *Entertainments For All Seasons* (1904) described this elegant treatment:

> She was dressed in a simple gown of pure white, an embroidered fichu crossing low over the front of her neck. A blue ribbon belt with a double bow of blue and red falling low over the skirt's graceful draperies, a knot of blue and red ribbon also at the throat of her bodice, and a red rose in her hair made her dress complete.

Even those who preferred not to invest in special attire could show patriotic spirit by wearing festive party hats made of cardboard and crepe or tissue papers. Many such chapeaux, like the smart lithographed cardboard "parade hats" with expanding tricolor tissue-paper honeycomb crowns that were advertised at *"three for ten cents"* in a 1904 Sears catalog, were made well enough to be saved to be worn at Fourth of July events for years to come.

PATRIOTIC FINERY FOR ALL OCCASIONS

* "When the guests arrived the ladies received liberty caps made of red, white and blue tissue paper and the gentlemen tall white paper 'Uncle Sam' stovepipes with broad bands of the red, white and blue." (*The Harvey Tribune-Citizen*, June 24, 1904)

* "There is nothing as charming in the way of dress as simple white with blue ribbons at the belt, in the hair and as a corsage finish to the slightly low bodice. A few sprays of salvia worn in the hair carries out the color scheme." (*Entertainments For All Seasons*, 1904)

* "An Uncle Sam disguise always provokes much merriment for . . . parties, especially when authentically carried out. The trousers are made of red and white striped material, the coat of blue with white stars cut out and sewed on, and collar and revers of red and white stripe. The dickey is also striped red and white of smaller design; the collar is white and the tie dark blue with white polka dots. A skull cap is given to which the hair may be

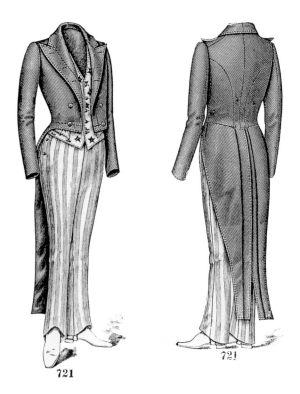

"The suit represented is the one always given to Uncle Sam, although cut upon more graceful lines and showing perfect adjustment." Illustrations of Uncle Sam costume Butterick Pattern No. 721 (The Delineator, October 1898).

sewn, or a wig may be worn." (*The Designer*, October 1913)

* "Ask [the children] to come dressed patriotically. Boy Scout suits and Red Cross Nurse costumes are easiest, as almost every boy and girl has one." (*The Children's Party Book*, 1924)

* "The guests wore patriotic costumes, the ladies being in white with red, white and blue sashes and stock, while the gentlemen wore ties to correspond, and tiny flags in their buttonholes." (*Entertainments For All Seasons*, 1904)

* *A Fourth-of-July Party for the Children.* "The little hostess is dressed in white, with a sash and hair-ribbons of red, white and blue stripes. As the guests arrive they are each decorated with a small silk flag." (*McCall's Magazine*, 1913)

* "'Columbia,' who is the reader of the verses, should be costumed for the part. A blue muslin waist may be covered with tinsel stars. Her skirt may be flags draped over a skirt of blue, or she may have a round skirt made of several inexpensive flags." (*The Household*, July 1902)

* "Each of the guests may be presented with a tricolored tissue-paper cocked-hat to wear. If they came in Colonial costumes it would add very much to the scene." (*The Delineator*, July 1908)

* "All citizens are requested to wear boutonnieres of red, white, and blue on the Fourth. Florists have been requested to order large quantities of red and white carnations, and a plan will be evolved to put [dyed] blue carnations on the market." (*The New York Times*, June 13, 1910)

* "Standing at one end of the long table they will see Miss Columbia in a long white robe with a flag draped about her head, and a large flag in her right hand resting on its staff." (*Entertainments For All Seasons*, 1904)

"This Greek-inspired dress is most suitable for Miss Liberty; the Phrygian cap as seen in the illustration is one of the oldest symbols of liberty." Illustrations of Miss Liberty costume Butterick Pattern No. 723. (The Delineator, *October 1898*).

Lady's and child's patriotic crepe paper costumes (Dennison's Party Book, *1922*).

Automobiles and Trucks in Gala Array

Excerpted from Dennison's *How to Decorate Halls, Booths and Automobiles,* 1923

The most attractive feature of many a community celebration is the parade, and the section of the parade which calls forth the most comments is the one of decorated automobiles.

Fringed crepe and crushed crepe are very effective and easily arranged. In most cases several rows of short fringe will be more satisfactory than a very deep fringe [that may be] blown out of place when the car is in motion.

Usually the first thing to do . . . is to cover [the vehicle] with pieces of cambric over the hood and tie them to the hood fastenings; then put pieces around the body of the car, tying, pinning, or sewing in place. Gummed cloth tape can [also be used].

The wheels are often entirely covered. The easiest way to do this is to cut a circle of cardboard the size to fit inside the rim. Cut an opening in the center to fit around the hub. Attach fine wires at the required distances around the edge to fasten to the spokes. Be careful to select designs the effect of which will not be lost when the wheels are in motion.

Sometimes simple decorations may be arranged for which no cloth foundation will be necessary. [An open-top] car [may be] quickly arranged using festoons, flags and patriotic shields. The festoons are pinned tightly around the bumper and will have to be attached to the windshield either with gummed tape or to a wire which has been stretched tightly around the top of the glass. Miniature festoons are fastened to each spoke of the wheels.

"Suggestions for the Holiday Parade," crepe paper decorations for cars (Dennison's Party Book, 1921).

"The car beautiful: fringe makes a very good foundation for an automobile trim," crepe paper decorations for a parade car (Dennison's Party Book, 1916).

A Patriotic "Special"

From Dennison's *Party Book*, 1921

This illustration shows how a plain slip-over foundation may be trimmed very attractively with three ruffles cut and sewed on one above the other.

Any motif cut from decorated crepe paper may be pasted on the front of the waist with good effect. Here we have a shield and eagle cut from [decorative] Crepe Paper No. P557.

The hat is simply two big squares of crepe paper pasted together to give firmness, with a soft crown added which fits the head. Stars constitute the trimming.

MEMORIES OF THE
"NEW AND MORE GLORIOUS" FOURTH

A Photo Album

"The Fourth is THE best day for a parade . . . even if you do have to start it yourself." Vintage photograph ca. 1920.

"I just knew that Edith and Roger would copy our costumes again this year." Early-twentieth-century photograph.

"Don't we all look so-o-o cute in these little flag frocks?" Vintage real-photo postcard. Postally unused with salutation on reverse.

"Ready?. . . Set? . . . Parade!!" Vintage photograph ca. 1915.

"Look, Rolfie boy . . . the parade is sure to start any minute now." Vintage real-photo postcard. Postally unused.

"It really IS a grand old flag, isn't it?" Vintage real-photo postcard. Mailed Fridley, Montana, April 17, 1908.

"What a beautiful day for an outing." Vintage photograph endorsed "Picnic Party July 4th 1891" on reverse.

"I wish it was the Fourth o' July every day." Early-twentieth-century photograph with the name "Sonny Pomeroy" written on reverse.

LET US ENTERTAIN YOU

Party Games and Other Amusements

"'How shall we celebrate the Fourth of July?' is a question that is asked in almost every home throughout the United States during the week previous to the coming of Independence Day. A need is often felt of some additional attraction to make the day a perfect one. . . . Almost invariably there comes a gap in the day's celebration; a time in the afternoon when the supply of fireworks set apart for the day-time has been exhausted, and when it is still too light to think of commencing the [evening displays]. It is then that the children begin to ask fretfully, 'What shall we do next?'"
McCall's Magazine, July 1909

"Something going all the time" was the battle cry of those charged with planning activities at turn-of-the-twentieth-century gatherings. In the case of the safe and sane "New and More Glorious Fourth," though, the party games and amusements themselves were recruits in the movement to replace fireworks with more sensible holiday activities.

Diversions designed for adults were likely to include games, usually of the variety that required participants to perform stunts or "forfeits" of a silly or comical nature, and music. Listening to live music at outdoor venues, dancing near the town bandstand, and gathering around the parlor piano to sing patriotic tunes were all popular Fourth of July pastimes.

People also engaged in forms of group theatre, as was the case with performances of a "living flag." An interactive patriotic tribute of this sort could be staged by assembling several hundred people in a venue with stadium-style seating and arranging for each participant to don a matching cap and cape preselected to be either red, white, or blue. Each of those designated blue also held a single oversized star made of white cardboard. When everyone reported to his or her strategically determined seat and the assemblage was

*Vintage embossed postcard marked "No. 51666."
Mailed Worcester, Massachusetts, July 10, 1909.*

*Vintage embossed postcard marked "Fourth of July Series
No. 2." Mailed New Palestine, Indiana, June 27, 1910.*

viewed at a distance, it resembled an ersatz American flag of gigantic proportions.

Activities for children almost always engaged them in some physical fashion and youngsters were kept busy with safe and sane confetti-and-ribbon battles, flag drills, hide-and-seek games, and performance-related activities such as pageants, pantomimes, and recitations. Lively games of croquet were played either outdoors in familiar lawn settings, or indoors using diminutive tabletop sets.

Arts and crafts projects also served as party amusements for the younger set. To this end, *McCall's Magazine* (1912) suggested that the little ones make their own "soldier hats" using brown wrapping paper and long strips of red, white, and blue tissue paper. A matching badge of red, white, or blue "kindergarten" (construction) paper and decorated with silver stars completed an outfit that was perfect for an impromptu parade.

One fascinating and extremely popular Independence Day practice involved launching fire balloons, intriguing instruments of nighttime flight that were propelled upward by varied sources of hot air. There indeed were tricks to designing a balloon of flight-worthy shape, but for the most part, the ethereal airships could be made at home in most any manageable size desired, large or small.

Fire balloons were often excluded from the fireworks restrictions enacted in the early 1900s. Due to the unpredictability of their flight patterns, however, the balloons did pose substantial danger to anything or anyone beneath. Any balloons that didn't disintegrate in a relatively safe fashion were still capable of igniting fires when they eventually *did* plummet to earth. Nevertheless, the mesmerizing effects of these glowing airships gliding ever higher into the night sky were yet another of the fanciful customs that helped make the Fourth of July ever glorious once-upon-an-old-fashioned time.

PARTY AMUSEMENTS

* "[Using] several streamers of red, white and blue crepe paper, dress each child for [a] 'tin-pan' parade. It is surprising how effective a simple sash, cap or regalia can be. From an array of

tin pans, plates, forks, spoons, toy drums, horns and whistles, let each parader select his favorite instrument. Tune and tone matter not to this wandering band, the only requisite is *NOISE*, and plenty of it!" (Dennison's *Children's Parties,* 1928)

* "After the ice cream, cake and punch are served, each guest is called upon to give a quotation, a bit of verse, or make a speech. Humorous and patriotic sentiments are often combined, and the hour will be spent pleasantly in this manner." (*Entertainments For All Seasons,* 1904)

* "The guests were invited to take part in a Liberty pole dance, and it was a pretty sight to see the red, white and blue streamers being wound around the pole." (*The Designer,* July 1903)

* "A few dances on the green also add a delightful finish to the evening when the few fireworks have slid their fiery path across the sky. The old-time Virginia reel, 'up the middle and down again,' is more adapted to the grassy dancing hall; and with the little merry bursts from the ranks of the stately dance into the gayer waltz or two-step, makes a pretty scene, under the lantern-lit trees and the star-lit sky, the charm of which is felt even by the dancers themselves." (*Entertainments For All Seasons,* 1904)

* "After supper was over, the strains of the piano from within the house floated out, and we all sang the 'Star Spangled Banner,' 'My Country, 'tis of Thee,' and other patriotic airs, until the shadows lengthened, the stars came out and the night was born." (*The Ladies' World,* July 1903)

PARTY GAMES

* The children would enjoy pinning the stars into the blue field of a flag drawn on a curtain. The feat is performed with eyes shut or bandaged. All those who succeed in placing their stars are eligible to draw for a prize." (*The Book of Frolics,* 1911)

* "Then all were seated on cushions under the historic tree, and within a circle of giant fire-crackers, attached in such

Vintage postcard marked "1166." Postally unused.

Vintage embossed postcard marked "American Post Card 'Independence Day' Series No. 124, Subject No. 2315, Published by the Ullman Manufacturing Co." Mailed Petaluma, California, July 2, 1914.

a manner that one frequently exploded. An historic tale was started by the hostess with the first explosion, and as the next cracker went off a second took up the narrative, and a third and fourth in the same manner, each introducing a new historical character and maintaining a connection until the last firecracker had exploded." (*Entertainments For All Seasons*, 1904)

* "Begin the fun with a Flag Search, with flags big and little hidden in the grass and vines or caught in the lower limbs of the trees and shrubbery. Inaugurate the hunt with a lively tattoo beaten on a drum. Allow twenty minutes for the flag search, and award a silk flag as a prize to the one finding most." (*The Designer*, July 1913)

* "A laughable blindfold game lies in furnishing Uncle Sam with his familiar goatee. A likeness of the good uncle (a very crude one will serve) is drawn or painted on a square of muslin which is afterwards stretched taut on a wooden frame. An unused picture frame is good for this. The beards are made of raveled manila rope and each person in turn endeavors to furnish 'Uncle Samuel' with a hirsute appendage. An Uncle Sam bonbonniere filled with chocolates would make an acceptable gift for a prize-winner of either sex." (*The Book of Frolics*, 1911)

* *Government Red Tape.* "The 'Entertainment Ball' for this occasion is simply a large ball made of wide red tape into which at intervals have been wound papers naming certain stunts which guests are obliged to perform. The ball is passed around the circle to the left and each guest unwinds until he reaches a paper. All the stunts, riddles, conundrums, poems to be read, songs to be sung, should pertain to national affairs." (*Parties All the Year*, 1923)

* "[This is] an entertaining game to play on the porch . . . and one that has an educational value as well. The puzzle is made up of the U.S. cut out on state lines. Not one person in a hundred can place the states of the United States in their proper relation to each other, and it is interesting to see how far wrong the participants in this game may go." (*The Ladies' Home Journal*, July 1914)

* "The game of Ten Pins can be [called] 'Fire Cracker' [and played using] shaped pins of wood painted bright red with little wires inserted at the top to simulate fuses. The balls used can be ordinary ones of wood stained black to represent cannon balls." (*The Housekeeper*, July 1908)

* "One humorous game consists in seeing who can draw the best representation of an American flag with his eyes shut." (*The Book of Frolics*, 1911)

* "Suspend a bell in a doorway low enough for the children reach. The children stand about ten feet away and each in turn throws a beanbag, endeavoring to make the 'liberty bell,' as it is called, ring. Those who succeed receive little bells as a reward." (*Games For Everybody*, 1905)

* "A very nice way to celebrate the Fourth would be to have a history match. All the children invited should find out as much about the Revolutionary War as they could. Judges should decide who was the winner. The one who told the most should be presented with a picture or a biography of Washington." (Eleven-year-old Frances Brookman writing for the "Children's Hour" page of *The Housekeeper*, July 1904)

* *A Liberty Pole.* "Erect a pole surmounted by a huge liberty cap, from which muslin streamers of red, white and blue stretch in every direction. To these pin slips of paper containing different lines of one patriotic song. Each guest finds his or her partner as the one holding the complement of the line drawn. When the poem is completed, ring a bell and all stand round the pole and sing the song itself." (*The Designer*, July 1912)

* "Invite your guests each to impersonate one of the presidents or his wife by wearing a sign which is presented by the hostess. The game is to arrange the presidents in proper order, and to match each to his wife." (Dennison's *Party Book*, 1921)

* "Now let the hostess produce a flower-pot or a little box with a flag embedded in the earth. Each player in turn

Vintage embossed postcard marked "Fourth of July Series No. 4." Postally unused.

Vintage embossed postcard marked "Fourth of July Series No. 2." Postally unused with salutation on reverse.

Vintage embossed postcard with shiny "gelatin" finish marked "0684." Mailed Lewiston, Maine, July 4, 1913.

endeavors to take away a spoonful of the earth or sand without overthrowing the flag. [Any player] who overthrows the flag must perform some comic feat imposed by the others, while all those who avoid this mishap are entitled, when the pot is empty, to draw for a prize." (*The Designer*, July 1913)

FETING THE FOURTH IN RHYME AND SEASON

"And so [when] it comes that in casting about for a means of stamping the import of the term Liberty upon the mind of Young America, and kindling in his breast the first spark of patriotism, it is the wise mother who falls back upon the home celebration, and thus effectually intertwines with Columbia's stirring anthems the refrain of 'Home, Sweet Home.' If she would have her children grow to be loyal patriots, let her make much of the Fourth in her home circle; let the house be brave in the Stars and Stripes . . . which every child should early learn to recognize . . . let music and merrymaking hold sway; let special menus be arranged; in short, let everything be employed which will tend to impress the significance of The Day We Celebrate."

The Ladies' World, July 1908

It should come as no surprise that in an era when people truly appreciated sweet sentiment and expressed it at every turn in their attitudes, manners, and accoutrements, poetry was considered a part of everyday living. Publications of every type offered their readers evocative words and couplets designed to enhance their perspectives on the world around them.

Though popular throughout the year, poems with patriotic themes were especially savored on and around the Fourth of July. In addition, verse that succeeded in putting a mirthful, if not entirely cautionary, spin on the joyful noise that could be heard here, there, and everywhere on the Glorious Fourth did its part in capturing the merry spirit of the day. Either way, Americans in the early twentieth century were regaled with Independence Day rhymes like these.

CELEBRATING THE DAY IN POEM

A Fourth of July Record
The Designer, July 1901

1 was a wideawake little boy who rose at the break of day;
2 were the minutes he took to dress, then he was off and away;
3 were his leaps which cleared the stairs, although they were steep and high;
4 was the number which caused his haste, because it was *The Fourth of July!*
5 were the pennies which went to buy a packet of crackers red;
6 were the matches which touched them off, and then—he was back in bed.
7 big plasters he had to wear to cover his burns so sore;
8 were the visits the doctor made before he was whole once more;
9 were the dolorous days he spent in sorrow and pain, but then
0 are the seconds he'll stop to think before he does it again.

The Liberty Bell
By Mary Lee Dalton, *The Youth's Companion,* June 29, 1916

The bell that pealed its tidings out, that July long ago,
No longer from the belfry beams is swinging to and fro;
Its iron tongue is silent now in Independence Hall,
And yet it sends its message far, and you can hear its call.

For when, upon the Glorious Fourth, they ring each brazen bell,
The old bell's voice is in them all, if you but listen well.
"Our land is free; oh, keep it free!" the message peals along.
"Let every true American be just and brave and strong!"

Vintage embossed postcard marked "Fourth of July Series No. 3." Postally unused.

Freddie, His Finger, and the Firecracker
(Being a Tale of the Fourth of July)
By EdgarWade Abbot, *Outlook,* July 7, 1894

This tale is a story of July the fourth,
    And the trouble that happened to Freddie:
Who held in his hand a great big piece of punk,
    And said, "Are you fellows all ready?"

And this is the finger done up in a rag,
    I tell you it takes lots of spunk
Not to howl and get mad when you touch off your thumb
    (Instead of the cracker), with punk.

A Thankful Woman
By Cora A. Matson Dolson,
New Idea Woman's Magazine, July 1907

It is 10 P.M. on the Fourth of July,
    And a thankful woman indeed am I.
With my seven-years' boy asleep on my knee,
    I'm thankful as only a mother can be.
He's burned his fingers and lost his hat,
    And torn his trousers—but what of that?
For a house, and a barn, and a boy have I . . .
    And a year away is next Fourth of July.

Vintage embossed postcard marked "753." Postally unused.

An Old Virginia Fourth
By Minna Irving, *The Designer,* July 1905

I'd like to keep the Fourth, Sir, as once we used to do,
    Way down in old Virginia, when we gave a barbecue;
And all the maidens pretty as bonnets in a box

Came trooping in for miles around to help us eat the ox.

I smell the roasted chickens, and see the tables spread,
  With flags and bunting streaming from the branches
  overhead.
I hear again the music, when the ringing, swinging beat
  Of "Dixie" mounted to our heads, and got into our feet.

When everybody shouted for the "Red, White and Blue,"
  Our voices drowned the drumming as we sang the
  chorus through.
And we all went homeward humming its patriotic bars,
  With rockets dropping from the sky a shower of crimson
  stars.

Josie's Point of View
The Youth's Companion, July 4, 1901

The Fourth may be a merry time,
  But give us the Third, I cry!
You need not worry 'bout dreadful boys.
  And catching on fire and deafening noise;
The punk doesn't burn a hole in your gown
  When you just for an instant lay it down;
But you buy your crackers, torpedoes and caps,
  And land them over without mishaps
On the pleasant Third of July!

The Day After
By Edwin L. Sabin, *The Household*, July 1901

'Twas the day after Fourth of July; and a sight
  Was Reginald William Cadwallader Wright!
All bandaged, and plastered, and forced to lie still,

Vintage postcard marked "Copyright 1907 G.W. Hull & Co." Postally unused.

Vintage embossed postcard marked "S129." Postally unused.

A regular mummy was Reginald Will
While as for his features—indeed, it was hard
    To see them, because of the linen and lard!

A "fizzer" (which fizzed much too soon, I suppose)
    Had blistered the tip of his poor little nose.
A rocket, by acting exceedingly queer,
    Had carried to Saturn a half of one ear.
A giant firecracker refusing to go,
    This Reginald bent o'er the fuse, close, to blow—
But sad to announce (tho' the truth must be known)
    'Twas Reginald William himself, who was blown!
And when he reached earth again, lo, I declare
    He was minus his eyebrows and more of his hair;
His cheeks and his forehead with powder
were specked,
    Like a cooky with caraway seeds well bedecked.

A cracker he held, as he'd seen others do—
    And when it went off, why, a finger went, too!
Besides, in his pocket a bunch, they relate,
    Began to explode at a terrible rate,
While Reggie ran prancing and dancing about
    Until he was soaked with the hose, and put out.

And, oh, he had sat on some punk, burning bright,
    Had Reginald William Cadwallader Wright!
Yet (would you believe it!), I heard this boy say
    He wished it were Fourth of July ev'ry day!

July 4
The Youth's Companion, July 4, 1894

On the Fourth of July long ago,
    That honored and fortunate day,
Our ancestors boldly said "No!"
    To the stranger's imperious sway.

*Vintage postcard marked "Copyrighted 1908 H.M. Rose."
Mailed Ionia, Michigan, June 24, 1909.*

*Vintage heavily embossed postcard marked "PFB
Series 8461." Postally unused.*

Vintage embossed postcard marked "No. 746." Postally unused.

II.

And undaunted by hardship and pain,
  Those sturdy old heroes declared
Independence they all would maintain,
  And bravely for battle prepared.

III.

And long shall our chronicles tell
  On that glorious page of the past.
How our fathers fought nobly and well
  And our fetters were broken at last.

IV.

So now on the Fourth of July
  Let children and elder folk, too,
To that old voice of freedom reply
  With a cheer for the Red, White and Blue.

July Fourth
By Nancy Byrd Turner,
The Youth's Companion, June 29, 1916

Oh, the glorious racket,
  How it thrills a chap—
Rockets shooting, pin wheels scooting,
  Here and there and everywhere
Snap! Snap! Snap!

Band around the corner
  Making heartstrings hum,
Cornet fluting, trombone tooting;
  Hear the drum as they come,
Br-r-rum bum bum!

Marching, laughing, shouting,
  Cheering near and far;
Boy and man, American.
  Whooping for America—
Hip-hip-hurrah!

Ted's Fourth of July
By Maud Osborne, **St. Nicholas Magazine**, July 1907

F—ourth of July!" said our mischievous Ted;
O—h, but I've planned to have bushels of fun;
U—p in the morning, by five, out of bed,
R—eady to fire off my cannon and gun.
T—hen I've a thousand torpedoes and wheels,
H—undreds of whirligigs, fizzers, and reels—

O—ceans of crackers, confetti, and slings,
F—unny old dragon-shaped Japanese things!

J—ust you keep watch while my sky-rockets soar
U—p in the air with a whirr and a whiz;
L—arge roman-candles, a dozen or more,
Y—ou'll see a-hissing and whirling their fizz!

1 day to wait was too long for our lad,
9 cannon crackers he fired (luckless Ted!)
0—n the Third. But his burns they were fearfully bad—
7 days from the Third Teddy spent in his bed!

Hats Off!
The Harvey Tribune-Citizen, June 24, 1904

Hats off, boys, to the flag floating high!
    How brightly it gleams 'neath the blue of the sky.
Hats off, boys, to the colors upborne!
    They are victory's emblem of right over wrong.

Hats off, boys, to the flag floating high!
    Proudly it waves for the Fourth of July.
Hats off, boys, for the loyalty true
    Which lives in each fold of the red, white and blue!

Vintage embossed postcard marked "S129." Mailed New York, New York, Station S, July 1, 1910.

Vintage postcard marked "Copyrighted Sandford Card Co. 1910." Postally unused.

Vintage embossed postcard marked "Fourth of July Series No. 4." Postally unused.

Vintage postcard marked "Copyrighted 1908 by Franz Huld Company." Mailed Syracuse, New York, June 30, 1908.

The Patriots
By Eunice Ward, *St. Nicholas Magazine*, July 1908

The burly cannon-cracker to the slender little flag
    Said, "How are *you* to celebrate the day?
You never make a single sound, you cannot jump nor shoot,
    And where they put you, there you have to stay."

The rockets, Roman candles, and the giddy, racy wheels
    With patriotic zeal began to brag.
Of how they'd leap and bang and fizz and flare and whirl—and all
    United to deride the silent flag.

But when the day was done, the crackers lay in scattered shreds;
    And bits of wheel were clinging to the trees;
The rocket sticks were lying prone; but high above the scene,
    The little flag still frolicked with the breeze.

A Dog's Fourth of July
By Arthur Ward, *The Ladies' World*, July 1899

Poor Bruno does not love the Fourth,
    To him it's never fun;
He's like our cat, it gives her fits,
    To only see a gun.

All day the crackers will explode,
    They snap all 'round his tail,
Till really if he wasn't black
    You'd see him turning pale.

And on that day, when bells are rung,
    His nose he puts up high,
And make a noise so loud you'd think
    He was about to die.

But when he finds the bells keep on,
    He droops his tail and ears,
And mournfully he trots away
    And quickly disappears.

Beneath his master's bed he hides,
    And neither eats nor drinks,
But through the day and through the night
    He simply lies and blinks.

But on the morning of the fifth
    He rushes out with joy,
And jumps and barks and plays about,
    As gay as any boy.

If Bruno was allowed a vote,
    And could just have his way,
I'm pretty sure there wouldn't be
    An Independence Day.

The Fourth
By Lindsay G. Lucas,
St. Nicholas Magazine, July 1923

Hurrah for Independence Day,
    When banners wave aloft!
The columns march in grand array,
    While cannons thunder oft!

We're up at dawn, in quest of larks,
    To add our own salute,
To join the throngs which fill the parks
    And hear the martial flute.

How grand it is throughout the day
    To hear the crackers bang!
The bells peal forth their tidings gay,
    As Liberty once rang!

Illustrated Fourth of July poem (The Chicago Heights Star, *July 1, 1909*).

And in the darksome eventide,
  The rockets flare on high,
While gay balloons, aglow inside,
  Go coursing o'er the sky.

  And still the peal and volley clear
Are heard to south and north.
  There is no day in all the year
Just like the jolly Fourth.

"Bobby Brown's Thought," illustrated poem (Little Folk's Monthly Magazine, *July 1910*).

Vintage thin cut-out "magic" postcard marked "Copyright 1906 by American Examiner" and "Compliments of Boston Sunday American." Directions on front of card reads "Heat up this Post Card with Hot Flat-iron, gas jet or match (Don't burn it)." Postally unused.

IT WAS A
GRAND OLD DAY

"In any case, no one old enough to remember such a Fourth of July is likely to forget, as long as he lives, the excitement of the dawn awakening, the wonderful pungent smell of gunpowder filling the air, the unaccustomed leniency of parents, the mood of a young nation innocently exulting in its strength and freedom, the glitter of the carnival, the beauty of colored flame burning against the great backdrop of night."

Recollections of the Fourth of July, ca. 1920
American Heritage Magazine, June 1959

"The end of a Perfect Day"

Vintage embossed postcard marked "Fond Memories Series No. 246." Postally unused.

RESOURCE GUIDE

ACKNOWLEDGMENTS

Party decorating ideas and illustrations from issues of Dennison's *Party Book, Gala Book, Patriotic Decorations and Suggestions, Children's Parties, Art and Decoration in Crepe & Tissue Paper,* and *How to Decorate Halls, Booths and Automobiles* have been photographed by the author from her own collection and have been reprinted with permission from the Avery Dennison Corporation.

ABOUT THE EMPHEMERA

Dedication page: Vintage postcard marked "1375." Mailed Baltimore, Maryland, Meade Branch, October 14, 1918.

Diminutive festive gummed seals appearing on pages 9, 12, 14-15, 23-24, 35-36, 40, 47, 51-52, 54-55, 63-65, 73, 89-90, 93-95, 99, 104-16, and 126 were manufactured by Dennison ca. 1910s-20s.

Diminutive festive gummed seals appearing on pages 96-98 were manufactured by Dennison ca. 1930s-40s.

Patriotic page-top border appearing on pages 7, 36, and 64 is from Dennison's *Party Book,* 1917.

Decorative edge appearing on page 15: Three embossed vintage postcards/same series marked "S.B. 258." All postally unused; backs of top and center cards each bear handwritten greetings on reverse.

Decorative edge appearing on page 24: Three embossed vintage postcards/same series marked "S 129." Top card postally unused with handwriting on reverse; center card mailed Long

Vintage postcard with shiny "gelatin" finish. Postally unused.

Island City, New York, no date; bottom card postally unused.

Decorative edge appearing on page 40: Three embossed vintage postcards/same series marked "Fourth of July Series No. 5." All postally unused.

Decorative edge appearing on page 52: Three embossed vintage postcards/same unmarked series. First card mailed Indianapolis, Indiana, July 4, 1911; remaining cards postally unused.

Decorative edge appearing on page 55: Three embossed vintage postcards/same series marked "J-8." First and third cards postally unused; middle card mailed Newburg, New York, July 3, 1912.

Decorative edge appearing on page 65: Three embossed vintage postcards/same unmarked series. First card mailed San Antonio, Texas, July 1, 1909; second card mailed Pompeii, Michigan, June 11, 1909; third card postally unused.

Decorative edge appearing on page 73: Three embossed vintage postcards/same unmarked series. Top card mailed New Athens, Illinois, June 4, 1913; center card mailed June 26, 1911, but city illegible; bottom card postally unused.

Decorative edge appearing on page 90: Three embossed vintage postcards/same series marked "752." All postally unused; top card has handwritten greeting on reverse.

Decorative edge appearing on page 99: Three embossed vintage postcards/same unmarked series. All postally unused; top and bottom cards have handwritten greetings on reverse.

Decorative edge appearing on page 105: Three embossed vintage postcards marked "Raphael Tuck & Sons' 'INDEPENDENCE DAY' Series of Post Cards, No. 109." Top card mailed Topeka, Kansas, July 4, 1910; center card mailed Edelstein, Illinois, July 3, 1908; bottom card mailed Kalamazoo, Michigan, June 12, 1910.

ABOUT THE COLLECTIBLES

Pin appearing on page 20: Vintage pin back, 1¼" diameter, commemorating the July 4, 1912, celebration sponsored by the Benton Park Safe and Sane Fourth Association.

Pin appearing on pages 31 and 96: Vintage pin back with embossed fabric flag attachment for "4th of July Celebration," NEWARK, July 4, 1916. Back endorsed "Allied Printing Rochester."

Decoration appearing on page 97: Vintage party cracker.

Box appearing on page 98: Package of Hitt's patented firecrackers.

Ribbon appearing on page 96: Double ribbon/double badge combination pin-on decoration. Center of eagle medal endorsed *"Fourth of July Celebration, Queens, N.Y. 1914"*; top metal bar endorsed *"3rd Vice President"*; white background ribbon endorsed *"Executive Committee."* Back endorsed *"F.F. Kummel Union Badge Maker, Local 11555 A.F. of I. Brooklyn."*

Badge appearing on page 98: Two-part metal badge. Upper portion endorsed *"Souvenir"*; lower portion endorsed *"Fourth July Celebration."* Back endorsed *"Schaab S&S Co. Milwaukee."*

Horn appearing on page 97: Cardboard horn with hand-crank ratchet device inside. Made by Marks Brothers Co.; bears patent date of Sept. 13, 1921.

Noisemaker appearing on page 97: Vintage 7" "Mama Horn" cardboard noisemaker, cries "ma-ma" when string is activated.

Box appearing on page 97: Box of Hitt's "Frashcrackas" ca. 1926.

BOOKS AND PERIODICALS

Abbott, Julie Wade. "Keeping School in the Home." *McCall's Magazine*, March 1912.

Anthony, Mary Louise. "Making a Library of Old Magazines." *The Designer*, April 1911.

Appelbaum, Diana Karter. *The Glorious Fourth: An American Holiday, an American History.* New York: Facts on File, Inc., 1989.

Ashton-Johnson, Carrie. "A Liberty Luncheon." *The Ladies' World*, July 1903.

Bartlett, John Russell, ed. *Records of the Colony of Rhode Island and Providence Plantations in New England.* Rhode Island: A.C. Greene and Brothers, 1859.

Beard, Lina, and Adelia B. *The American Girls Handy Book.* New York: Charles Scribner's Sons, 1890.

Beard, Mary Ritter. *Woman's Work in Municipalities.* New York: D. Appleton and Company, 1915.

Broome, Anne. "To Sup Electrically on the Fourth." *The Designer*, July 1916.

Brown, Edith S. "A Jolly Fourth of July Party." *McCall's Magazine*, July 1907.

Burt, Emily Rose. "Fourth-of-July Games." *McCall's Magazine*, July 1915.

——. "A Fourth-of-July Party for the Children." *McCall's Magazine*, July 1913.

Chilton, Anne. "An Independence Party." *Woman's Home Companion*, July 1920.

Chittenden, Alice. "A Fourth of July Luncheon." *The Modern Priscilla*, July 1902.

Coleman, Nellie G. "A Patriotic Lawn Party." *The Housekeeper*, July 1903.

Cowles, Julia Darrow. "The Children's Hour." *The Housekeeper*, July 1904.

Crane, Frank W. "The Old-Time 'Fourth.'" *Outlook*, June 20, 1896.

Crane, Helen Bertha. "Suggestions for Fourth of July." *The Household*, July 1901.

Cummings, T. Celestine. "A Firecrackerless Fourth for the Children." *New Idea Woman's Magazine*, July 1907.

McCall's Magazine, *July 1907.*

Dennison's Party Book, *1915.*

Curtis, George William. "Editor's Easy Chair." *Harper's New Monthly Magazine*, July 1854.

"Dainty Dishes for Fourth of July Dinner, Luncheon or Supper." *McCall's Magazine*, July 1906.

Dawson, Mary. "Come Rally Round the Flag." *The Designer*, July 1913.

——. "Fun for the Fourth of July." *The Designer*, July 1914.

——. "Patriotic Fun for the Fourth." *The Designer*. July 1915.

——. "A Red, White and Blue Party for Fourth of July." *The Designer*, July 1901.

Dawson, Mary, and Emma Paddock Telford. *The Book of Entertainments and Frolics For All Occasions*. Philadelphia: David McKay, 1911.

"Decorative Suggestions for the Fourth." *The Designer*, July 1911.

"Delicious Sandwiches for Picnics." *McCall's Magazine*, August 1910.

Dennison Manufacturing Co. Dennison's *Art and Decoration in Crepe & Tissue Paper*. Framingham, Mass.: Dennison Manufacturing Co., 1899, 1913.

——. *Children's Parties*. Framingham, Mass.: Dennison Manufacturing Co., 1928.

——. *Gala Book*. Framingham, Mass.: Dennison Manufacturing Co., 1922, 1923, 1925, 1926.

——. *How to Decorate Halls, Booths and Automobiles*. Framingham, Mass.: Dennison Manufacturing Co., 1923.

——. *Party Book*. Framingham, Mass.: Dennison Manufacturing Co., 1915, 1916, 1918, 1920, 1921.

——. *Patriotic Decorations and Suggestions*. Framingham, Mass.: Dennison Manufacturing Co. 1918.

Entertainments For All Seasons. New York: S.H. Moore & Co., 1904.

Fales, Winifred. "A Fourth of July Party." *The Delineator*, July 1907 and July 1908.

Fales, Winifred, and Mary H. Northend. *The Party Book*. Boston: Little, Brown, and Company, 1912.

"Fireworks is Wonder of All." *The New Castle News*, July 5, 1910.

"Fireworks Notice." *The Chicago Heights Star*, July 2, 1914.

Fitzgerald, Claudia M. *Parties All the Year*. New York: The McCall Co., 1923.

"Fourth of July Emergencies: What to Do When the Small Boy Hurts Himself." *The Delineator*, July 1908.

"A Fourth of July Entertainment." *The Household*, July 1902.

"A Fourth of July Party." *The Delineator*, July 1905.

"A Fourth of July Party." *The Harvey Tribune-Citizen*, June 24, 1904.

"A Fourth of July Without Fireworks." *The Ladies' Home Journal*, June 1907.

"The Fourth of July: An American Party." *McCall's Magazine*, July 1906.

"For the Picnic Menu." *The Ladies' World*, July 1896.

Fox, Genevieve. "Shall Your Safe Fourth be Stupid or Snappy?" *The Designer and The Woman's Magazine*, July 1922.

Frisbie, W.A. "How One City Had a Sane Fourth." *The Housekeeper*, July 1908.

Gale, Zona. "What Shall We Do with the Fourth of July?" *McCall's Magazine*, July 1913.

Gardner, Inez J. "How One Town Spends the Fourth." *The Ladies' Home Journal*, June 1908.

Gibson, Alice. "A Patriotic Poverty Party." *The Ladies' World*, July 1908.

Glassberg, David. *American Historical Pageantry: The Uses of Tradition in the Early Twentieth Century.* Chapel Hill: University of North Carolina Press, 1990.

Glenn, John M., Lilian Brandt, and F. Emerson Andrews. *Russell Sage Foundation 1907-1940: Volume One.* New York: Russell Sage Foundation, 1947.

"The Glorious Fourth." *The Housewife*, July 1914.

The Good Housekeeping Hostess. New York: The Phelps Publishing Co., 1904.

Goodnow, Ruby Ross. "A Community's Perfectly Glorious Fourth." *The Designer*, July 1915.

Gray, Helen S. "The Fourth as a National Nuisance." *The Ladies' Home Journal*, July 1907.

Griffin, Lillian Baynes. "A Sensible Fourth of July." *The Ladies' World*, July 1908.

Gunn, Lilian M. "The Picnic Shelf." *McCall's Magazine*, July 1920.

Heintze, James R. *The Fourth of July Encyclopedia.* Jefferson, North Carolina: McFarland & Company, Inc., 2007.

McCall's Magazine, *July 1905.*

The Housekeeper Magazine, *July 1908.*

Hofmann, May C. *Games for Everybody.* New York: Dodge Publishing Co., 1905.

"How to Carry Pie to a Picnic." *The Ladies' World,* July 1901.

"How We Celebrate the 4th in our Town." *The Ladies' World,* July 1913.

Howard, Frances, and Ella Evans. "A Half Dozen Entertainments: A Fourth-of-July Fete." *The Designer,* July 1903.

Hunt, Virginia. "A Fourth of July Party." *The Ladies' Home Journal,* July 1914.

"An Invitation to the Public." *The Chicago Heights Star,* June 24, 1909.

"Jack Horner Pies." *The Doll's Dressmaker Magazine,* January 1892.

Johnston, Grace M. "Games for a Safe and Sane Fourth." *The Designer,* July 1912.

Joy, Jane Ellis. "Patriotism—Its Quality and Expression." *The Mother's Magazine,* July 1910.

Judson, Helen A. "The Fourth-of-July Hostess." *The Designer,* July 1915.

"The Lady From Philadelphia Tells How to Entertain in the Country." *The Ladies' Home Journal,* July 1904.

Landes, Sarah W. "Menus in Patriotic Garb." *The Designer,* July 1902.

Lewis, [Mrs.] A. G. "Lawn Parties and Out-of-Door Fetes," *The Ladies' Home Journal,* July 1892.

Litwicki, Ellen M. *America's Public Holidays 1865-1920.* Washington: Smithsonian Institution Press, 2000.

Lucas, Eleanor M. "Fourth-of-July Dainties." *The Designer,* July 1904.

March, Marjorie. "A Cracker Party for Independence Day." *The Ladies' World,* July 1903.

———. "A Luncheon for the Fourth of July." *The Modern Priscilla,* July 1904.

———. "Patriotism and Fun Served with Crackers." *The Housekeeper,* July 1908.

Marchant, Eleanor. "A Stars-and-Stripes Entertainment." *The Designer,* July 1904.

Mathewson, Alice Clarke. "The Spirit of the Fourth." *The Delineator,* July 1917.

Megee, Katherine E. "Celebrating the Fourth in the Home." *The Ladies' World*, July 1908.

——. "A Fourth of July Breakfast Party." *The Housekeeper*, July 1904.

——. "A Fourth of July Luncheon." *The Household*, July 1901.

——. "For the Fourth of July." *The Ladies' World*, July 1901.

Mellot, Elizabeth. "Games and Entertainment for the Children on the Afternoon of the 4th of July." Dennison's *Children's Parties*, 1928.

Merriman, Faye N. "A Safe, Insane Fourth." *McCall's Magazine*, July 1917.

"Midsummer Menus." *The Designer*, July 1911.

Moore, [Mrs.] Sarah. "Dainties for the Fourth of July." *McCall's Magazine*, July 1908.

——. "Dainties for Fourth of July Spreads." *McCall's Magazine*, July 1910.

——. "Delicious Ice Cream and Water Ices." *McCall's Magazine*, July 1909.

Morrison, Elizabeth Wadsworth. "A Fourth of July Feast." *The Housekeeper*, July 1908.

——. "A Fourth of July Luncheon." *The Household*, July 1902.

Nathan, Ray Thum. "A Red, White and Blue Luncheon." *The Ladies' World*, July 1901.

"National Dress for Masquerade and Fancy Dress Parties." *The Delineator*, October 1898.

The New York Times:

"At 106 He Prefers a Noisy Fourth." July 5, 1910.

"Attractive Souvenirs of the Day." June 28, 1914.

"Big Trade in Fireworks." June 30, 1895.

"Boy Police Made an Orderly Fourth." July 1, 1907.

"Cincinnati's Safe Fourth." July 3, 1911.

"Day of Patriotism and Noise." July 4, 1893.

"Favors Citizenship Day." February 25, 1922.

"Features of the Holiday." July 6, 1897.

"Fireworks Makers Hard Hit by Gaynor." April 3, 1910.

"Fireworks in Plenty." June 14, 1895.

"Fourth Quiet Also in Other Cities." July 5, 1911.

"The Fourth of July." July 4, 1859.

"The Glorious Fourth Comparatively Quiet." July 5, 1901.

"How to Celebrate 'A Safe and Sane Fourth'—A Series of Contrasts." June 25, 1911.

Vintage postcard. Mailed Oneco, Connecticut, July 5, 1907.

McCall's Magazine, *July 1909.*

"An Ideal Fourth." July 3, 1873.

"Independence Day." July 4, 1854; July 7, 1858.

"July 4 Night Display." June 23, 1916.

"Less Noise, More Comfort." July 5, 1894.

"Like the Usual Holiday." July 5, 1885.

"Millions for Fireworks." June 28, 1891.

"Mrs. Smith's Grievances." July 25, 1884.

"New Fireworks for the Fourth of 1902." June 1, 1902.

"New York to Have a Lively Old Fourth." June 25, 1907.

"New York's Fourth to be a Gala Day." June 13, 1910.

"A Noisy Fourth of July." July 5, 1896.

"The Noisy 'Fourth.'" June 6, 1896.

"Roebling's Sane Fourth." July 3, 1909.

"Sane Fourth Story Book." June 23, 1916.

"Scenes in Fireworks Stores." July 4, 1894.

"Some Advice for the Fourth." July 1, 1894.

"'Twas the Usual Fourth." July 5, 1891.

"Whole City Joins in a Sane Fourth." July 5, 1910.

"Young America Ready for Fourth of July." July 3, 1901.

Nichols, Mary Ellis, and Grace E. Rutter. "A Patriotic Picnic for a Sane, Safe and Jolly Fourth of July." *The Designer,* July 1913.

Northend, Mary H. "Celebrating the Fourth." *McCall's Magazine,* July 1909.

——. "A Fourth of July Celebration Without Fireworks." *The Mother's Magazine,* July 1910.

——. "Patriotic Dishes for the Fourth." *McCall's Magazine,* July 1912.

Otis, Eleanor. "A Patriotic Picnic." *McCall's Magazine,* July 1914.

Page, Walter Hines, and Arthur Wilson. *The World's Work: A History of Our Time.* New York: Doubleday, Page & Co., 1913.

Parker, Marion Jane, and Helen Harrington Downing. *The Children's Party Book.* Chicago: Rogers & Co., 1924.

Parties for Children. McCall's Magazine, ca. 1920.

"Patriotic Affairs for the Fourth." *Woman's Home Companion,* July 1915.

Peck, Frances. "A Little Feast for the Fourth." *The Designer,* July 1906.

Pennybacker, [Mrs.] Percy V. "An Ideal Fourth of July." *The American City*, June 1922.

"Picnic-Giving." *The Delineator*, July 1894.

"The Picnic Basket." *Good Housekeeping Magazine*, July 1914.

"The Picnic Lunch Basket." *The Delineator*, July 1908.

Price, Hester. "The Table on the Fourth of July." *The Ladies' Home Journal*, July 1904.

Red Letter Day Parties. Topeka, Kans.: The Capper Farm Press, ca. 1920.

"Red, White, and Blue Entertaining." *McCall's Magazine*, October 1917.

Rittenhouse, Anne. "Entertaining on the Fourth of July." *The Delineator*, July 1908.

Rorer, [Mrs.] "A Fourth of July Dinner." *Good Housekeeping Magazine*, July 1914.

Rosenzweig, Roy. *Eight Hours for What We Will: Workers and leisure in an industrial city, 1870-1920.* Cambridge: Cambridge University Press, 1983.

Sackett, Ruth Virginia. "A Fourth-of-July Question Party." *The Designer*, July 1904.

Sanford, [Mrs.] Grace F. "Our Fourth of July Picnic." *The Ladies' Home Journal*, July 1904.

Smilor, Raymond W. "Creating a National Festival: The Campaign for a Safe and Sane Fourth, 1903-1916." *The Journal of American Culture*, Winter 1980.

Smith, Bradford. "The Glorious Unsafe Fourth." *American Heritage Magazine*, June 1959.

"Suggestions for Fourth of July Dinner and Menu Cards." *The Delineator*, July 1894.

Telford, Emma Paddock. "Fourth of July Luncheons and Dinners." *The Delineator*, July 1910.

——. "A Yankee Doodle Day for The Children." *The Designer*, July 1912.

Twitchel, Gertrude S. "July Entertainments: Patriotic affairs that are easily planned for the Fourth." *Woman's Home Companion*, July 1915.

"An Uncle Sam Costume of Authentic Dress." *The Designer*, October 1913.

Wallis, Claire. "A Glorious Fourth for Everyone." *McCall's Magazine*, July 1920.

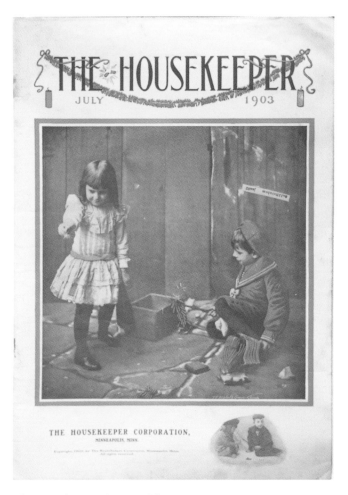

The Housekeeper Magazine, *July 1903.*

Vintage embossed postcard marked "International Art Publ. Co. Series No. 974." Mailed Elba, New York, July 2, 1910.

Warren, Charles. "Fourth of July Myths." *The William and Mary Quarterly,* July 1945.

Weaver, Louise Bennett, and Helen Cowles LeCron. *A Thousand Ways to Please a Husband with Bettina's Best Recipes.* New York: Britton Publishing Co., 1917.

Wolcott, Theresa Hunt. *The Book of Games and Parties For All Occasions.* Boston: Small, Maynard & Company, 1920.

Wright, Mary Mason. "A Page of Patriotic 'Eats.'" *The Designer and the Woman's Magazine,* July 1921.

——. "Patriotic Food for the Fourth." *The Designer,* July 1917.

Vintage postcard marked "Copyright 1907 Tower M&N Co., NY 106S-6." Mailed Sidney, Ohio, June 16, 1910.

Vintage embossed postcard marked "Copyright 1908 P. Sander, N.Y."
Mailed Clayton & Easton, T440, R.P.O. July 5, 1911.